Scrag - Up The H
Jesamine James
Based on a true story.

*Copyright© Jesamine James
First ebook edition 2013.
Published on behalf of the silent.*

*The characters and events portrayed in this book are fictitious.
Any similarity to real persons, living or dead, is not coincidental and intended by the author.*

All rights reserved. No part of this book may be reproduced, stored in a retrieval system or transmitted without written permission of the publisher.

Contents

Part 1	2010
	Fill Your Heart
	Sense of Doubt
	Breaking Glass
	Time
	Five years
	Blackout
Part 2	1981
	Changes
	Saviour Machine
	Sons of the Silent Age
	Memory of a Free Festival
	Rebel Rebel
	China Girl
	Ashes to Ashes
	Because you're Young
	Scary Monsters
	Starman

	Station to Station
	Move On
	Unwashed and Somewhat Slightly Dazed
	Fantastic Voyage
	The Width of a Circle
	All the Madmen
Part 3	2010
	Across the Universe
	Always Crashing in the Same Car
	Scream Like a Baby
	It's No Game
	After All
	Epilogue/Epitaph

Part 1 - Fill your Heart, 2010.

"Did you enjoy the show?" Colin asks, as we climb into the car.

"Yeah, I haven't laughed so much in years. I've never seen a live comedian before." I light a cigarette.

"Really, where've you been all your life? I'll have to take you out more often." He smiles at me with a look that suggests he is asking me on another date.

"I'd really like that," I whisper, as I open the window and flick the ash from my cigarette. We leave the car park. I can't look at him when I answer.

"We could always stop for a drink some place," I mention, as I watch the houses pass us by.

"Well, unless you want to go clubbing and feel like the oldest swinger in town, I suggest we do that another time. It's gone midnight you know. Some of us have to be up in five hours for work, and I've still got a half hour drive home."

"Really, that late? I'm sorry. I didn't realise. The time has gone so quickly." My cheeks flush in the dark, and I flick the cigarette out through the window; it didn't taste good.

I don't want to go home, not yet. An ancient teenage anxiety stirs in me, and not in a good way.

I always hate going home - not that there's anything wrong with my house - it's the going, the journey that stirs the nausea.

"I'll take that as a compliment. Now I know you enjoyed yourself," he replies.

I know he is smiling, and he has a beautiful smile. I should feel comfortable, but something is wrong. Something is wrong with me.

"Are you alright? You've gone very quiet," he asks, as he parks the car outside my house.

"Do you ever get the feeling that something really bad has happened?" I say, turning to face him.

"Yeah, once I went round my dad's. It was really windy and I suddenly had this thought that my dog was lost. I went straight home and found my garden fence had been blown down and the dog was gone. It was weird."

"Did you find him?"

"Yeah, too right I did. Someone had handed him in to the shelter. It cost me seventy quid to get him out. He'd only been there an hour or two, robbing bastards."

I chuckle because he swore. Something that I find hard not to do myself. It isn't enough to relieve the anxiety that's churning inside me though.

"I have a horrible feeling now," I say, as I open the car door.

He gently touches my arm and leans towards me. "I'll give you a ring tomorrow to see how you are, I'm sure everything will be fine."

"Thank you and thank you for a great evening. I hope we can do it again soon." I kiss him on the cheek catching the edge of his lips.

"You're trembling. Are you cold?" He looks concerned as he touches my cheek.

"I'll be fine." I pull away and scuttle out of the car.

He waits until I'm through my front door before driving away. He has to be the nicest person I've ever met in my whole life, and he is beautiful. It's a shame that he's called Colin; it's an old, uncool name, but we are old and uncool now, I suppose.

Far too awake to go straight to bed, I pour myself a vodka and lime to settle my nerves and my stomach. I do some writing into the early hours to wear myself out. I'm aware that I haven't had enough vodka and accept the inevitable. I hate going to sleep, but it is an unfortunate necessity. When my eyelids get heavy, I take myself up to bed, snuggle up under the duvet and slide into a deep sleep.

I can sense the heavy breathing close to my head. I'm aware that I definitely went to bed on my own, but it doesn't feel like my bed. I'm on a couch and it's wet. It dawns on me that I'm dreaming. I could try to wake myself, but that will take time. Time that I don't have. I resign myself to the fact that I'm going to have to deal with it quickly, again.

Something long and hard is pressing against my arse and digging into my back. I guess it's a baseball bat; it's usually close by. My small hand tightly grips around the bat before I open my eyes and leap up from the sodden couch. Richard is standing before me, naked. He looks surprised by my sudden reaction. Before he can react, I swing the baseball bat at him. It hits him sharply across the head, and as he loses his balance and teeters on one leg. I hit him again - this time in the bollocks - and he falls to the floor, scratching his way to the backdoor by his fingernails.

"Get out of my fucking house, you wanker!" I scream at him, as I swing the bat in his direction.

He struggles to his feet, stumbles and falls through the back doorway sneering, "I'll come back and I'll get you. I'll always come back." His eyes are deep in their sockets; they shine green and swell like they are trying to pop out. I know they can't, they've always been in too deep. I had tried ripping them out in a previous nightmare, and they turned into Brussels sprouts and made me retch. I could kill him, but it won't stop him returning.

I watch the naked Richard rise. He runs up the garden, jumps over the back gate and heads off up the street. He looks back and stares at me until he is out of view. As I close the door, I spot a lion that had been sleeping in the corner of the garden. It's watching me now with its ears pricked high.

"Shit, where's the fucking key? And why don't I wake up?" I mutter closing the door.

"Hello Marie."

I turn to see my uncle standing by the couch where Richard had been.

"You're dead," I shout at him.

"Don't be like that Marie. I've got some news for you," he continues.

"No! I meant you're really dead. I went to your funeral five years or so ago. Get out of my house and do up your flies." I grimace and look down in disgust at his exposed, shrivelled penis.

"Seriously, I have to talk to you," he continues without replacing his knob.

"I don't give a shit. I know you're dead and I'm dreaming, so just fuck off out of my house to wherever you came from." I don't want to hit him with the bat, but I grip it tightly ready for another shot.

There's a massive smash against the back door. The lion's huge head peers in through the broken glass. Uncle doesn't hang around any longer. He's out through the front door - his withered tackle still flapping outside his open fly.

I face the lion; it is intent on getting into the house. I need a gun not a baseball bat, so I flee as the lion continues to tear at the remainder of the back door with its claws.

Heading for the staircase, I leap and run up two at a time. Halfway up I'm brought to a halt; the top five stairs are missing. There's a sheer drop back down to the hallway. I can't risk trying to jump the gap. I won't get the height I need to reach the landing. The only option is to climb on to the banister rail. The rail is no wider than my small hands which seem to be getting smaller by the second, and my fingers fuse together like I'm wearing mittens.

I carefully climb up on to the banister rail and place one hand in front of the other. I inch my way along it like a caterpillar on a thin branch. I can see the lion below me in the hallway pacing back and forth. It is too stupid to think of looking upwards.

As I near the top, a warm breeze passes my face. I lift my head to see another bloody lion standing on the landing. It is watching the lion below intently - its tongue dripping with saliva.

I freeze, hold my breath and watch as my small hands, and the rest of my body, turn a mottled brown colour matching the shade of the banister rail that I'm perched upon. I merge into it - invisible. I am a chameleon.

The lion above me leaps forward, spanning the gap in the stairs with ease. With one more leap he lands on the lion in the hallway. The two lions engage in a vicious fight. Fur and blood fill the air, splatter the ceiling and walls. Loud roars of hatred and roars of pain echo through my house. In my camouflaged state, I continue to stay frozen and hold my breath in the hope that they'll kill each other and I can make my escape.

My mobile rings. Where is it? Do I even have any pockets? I can't tell. All I can see are my tiny clinging hands in front of me. The ringing sound is definitely coming from me.

The lions stop fighting distracted by the noise. They huff as they come up the stairs to investigate the strange, intrusive sound. I roll my right chameleon eye backwards and see the two blood-stained heads staring at me from the last stair. My phone keeps ringing. My hands are wringing wet with sweat, as I slowly slide backwards down the banister in my own perspiration. I am desperate to breathe, but I hold it in. I slide back further and further, and find myself out of the nightmare and returned to the safety of my own bed. I reach for my mobile, but the ring tone has stopped.

Breathing deeply for a while to catch the breaths that I'd held in, I check my surroundings. Everything looks normal, but I've had these nightmares before. They lead me into a false sense of security. I know I could be dreaming that I'm awake and soon the nightmare will continue.

Breath recovered, I pat dry the pool of sweat from between my breasts. My mind begins to unbewilder itself, as I hear the usual morning sounds from outside the house. I am content that I am truly awake.

I lie back to contemplate and interpret the last few minutes. The nightmares are always similar, but never the same. I'm startled as my mobile rings again.

"For fuck's sake," I cry out, nearly pissing myself. I reach over to answer it.

It's a call that I've been waiting for, for what seems like an eternity. The voice at the end of the line belongs to a police woman that I have come to know and trust over the past year. She asks if she can speak to Marie even though she knows it's me.

"Hello, yes it is Marie," I say rubbing my eyes. I don't want her to think that I've just woken up. I don't know why, as she can't see me.

"I thought you should know that we arrested Richard late last night. He was interviewed and charged. As he doesn't have an address, I'm pretty certain that he won't be released on bail…, Marie, are you still there?"

"Yes, yes of course I am. Sorry, it's a bit of a shock after all this time."

"Yes, it's taken a while, but we have him now. I can't tell you much more at the moment, but I'll keep you informed of any developments. Are you going to be okay? Have you got any questions?"

"I can't think of any right now. I'll be fine." I'll be fine - That is what I always say.

"Well you've got my number if anything comes to mind. I have to call the others now, take care."

"Cheers, bye." I hang up the phone. I have one missed call, from Colin. It must have been his call that had woken me from my nightmare. 'How uncanny, such a nice man,' I think, but I'm not going to call him back. I've always dealt with things on my own and no matter how much he cares, where would I begin anyway? My news isn't something I want to share with someone I hardly know.

So, I've received the news that I have waited so long for - Richard has finally been arrested. It has been a long two years attending interviews in police studios, answering questions and recalling things that didn't make sense to me at all at the time. I'd signed statements that were being written or taped as I spoke. All the time, other victims and witnesses had come forward and added their stories while I hadn't a clue that these other people had existed, or had suffered the same fate at Richard's deviancy. I was even filmed during one interview. That was a very strange experience. I'd kept wanting to smile for no apparent reason.

I am forty-two years old and I'm going to have to go to court and testify against him. I'll have to remember precisely and correctly the events of three decades ago. I knew this day would come, but I didn't know how I'd feel after hearing that news. For the first time in my life I can't explain the emotion. The fact that I have been taken seriously, and been believed, takes away the heavy pressure that weighed down on me and has always suppressed my willingness to speak up.

I had tracked Richard down myself. I found him living in a small town in Turkey. I'd given the police the address and a print out of Google Earth pinpointing his whereabouts. The police had tried everything possible to get him extradited, but had failed due to the time span of his crimes. All they could do was wait for him to leave the country to make their move. I truly believed that he would never leave. Now there's a question I should have asked her. I call Kate, the police woman, back.

"Hi Kate, it's Marie. I just wondered, how did you catch him?"

"We arrested him last night at his brother's house. He is apparently a very sick man and had to return for medical treatment. He'd been here a few weeks, and I'm surprised how he even got into the country without us being informed. Someone recognised him and reported him to us anonymously. That's all I can tell you at the moment."

"Thanks, at least you got him at last," is all I can think to say. I don't want to hear that he's very sick. I hope he dies, but I also hope he's not too sick to wangle himself out of going to court.

"Bye." I don't want to know any more.

I shower, dress and ponder the many questions that are spinning around in my head, questions that I don't want to bother Kate with.

What will happen next? What will it be like in court? Will I be interrogated? What should I wear? How long will it all take? What if I can't get the words out? I feel overjoyed and excited, but at the same time I'm scared and my insides churn with sick. Having an empty stomach, it burns at the back of my throat; I should eat something. I just can't face breakfast or filling the kettle with water. It is an emotional overload resulting in an emotional close down. I think I am going to puke up all the blackness that has been festering inside me for years. My legs are weak like I've walked a thousand stairs. I used to go to a small place in the back of my head and curl up into a ball at times like this, but I have learnt a very different way of dealing with it.

I pour myself a very large vodka with a very small amount of lime cordial; that fixes it. A good drink fixes everything; it helps me to sleep and stops me dreaming so much. It is the only solution when the nightmares come so often and become exhausting, that on waking up, I am more knackered than before I went to sleep. Hopefully this will be the turning point in my life and I can finally grow up.

I have tried for decades to forget, to eliminate, to erase it all from my memory. Suddenly, the most important thing to do in my life is to remember it all, all in its intimate and grotesque detail. It won't be difficult to recall. I know it is all in here still; it has always been in here. It is flashed back to me at the sound of a voice, at the whistling tune of the milkman, at the sell-by date on a piece of food, at the sight of a Brussels sprout, at the chiming of a clock, at the smell of sawdust and varnish, and it is all replayed to me during my sleep.

I can remember right back to the first time I encountered Richard.

Sense of Doubt

I first met Richard when I was six-years-old. My mum took me and my baby sister to a meeting group called the Gingerbread Club. This was a proper charity run club for single parents. It intended to help them and their children have a social life, and to meet others in similar situations. It wasn't so common in those days to be a single parent.

The club would organise swimming trips, picnics, days out at the zoo, more swimming trips - in fact we went on a hell of a lot of swimming trips - and any other place that would keep the kids happy. The adults could make friends with each other, find new partners or just enjoy the day out with their children. Richard was a recent widower, and he had a son. This was the only requirement necessary for membership to the Gingerbread group. Even as a six-year-old child, I pondered on the name of the group. It frightened the hell out of me, 'The *Gingerbread Club'*. The only thing that I knew about gingerbread was the Hansel and Gretel story and the Gingerbread man story. I'd never even tasted the stuff.

The Hansel and Gretel story is about two children who got lost in a forest and were lured and then imprisoned by a wicked witch in her kitchen. She wanted to cook them and eat them.

She lived in a house that was made of gingerbread and every sweetie imaginable, even the glass in the windows was made of sugar. She had tricked Hansel and Gretel into her house by pretending to be a nice, little old lady offering them sweets and goodies. I'm sure you are familiar with the tale.

Then there was the story of the gingerbread man. It was about a boy made lovingly out of gingerbread by an old couple. He ran away and ran through the whole book from every one he met. He ended up at a dead end with just an expanse of water in front of him. He hitched a lift on a fox's back, and halfway across the river the fox tossed his head up flinging the Gingerbread man into the air. He snapped his jaws and ate the little boy.

I couldn't understand why someone decided to call a support group for single parents and their children by such a sinister name. As a child I feared I would be kidnapped, thrown into an oven and eaten. The events of the following years did not prove me far wrong.

The court won't want to hear about Hansel and Gretel, my Gingerbread man or my enquiring childhood imagination. They want truth and evidence, so I have to get back into my real memory. The memory of relevant events that occurred.

The first time I'd encountered 'The' Richard, the one that I know, was when I was about seven years old and I had contracted German measles (apparently). I wasn't allowed to go to school. I would normally have stayed at home on my own - watching the television on the sofa all day - if I was too poorly to go to school. My mum would go to work as usual. That day Richard convinced her that this was irresponsible of her and illegal. He insisted on me going to stay at his house for the day.

He told my mum that he'd look after me and not to worry. He didn't go to work, so it wouldn't be much of a problem to him. She left me at his door and shot off in her silly bubble car.

He took me into the lounge. "It's nice and warm in here. You can lie on the couch. I'd better close the curtains - did your mum not tell you that the sun is very dangerous when you have German measles? You could go blind." As the room darkened I sat on the couch and shook my head. The television clicked to life and shed a little light around his silhouette that grew with each of his steps towards me.

"Right, you should wear these to be on the safe side." A pair of sunglasses were pushed on to my face before he adjusted the cushions and lifted my legs forcing me to lie on the couch. "You'll probably fall asleep soon. If you need anything just shout. I've got some jobs to do, but I'm not going out today." He smiled and put his hand on my forehead. "Erm, you do have quite a high temperature. I might have to get a doctor out. Do you have a rash?" Before I could answer he had lifted my dress above my knees. "Oh, you do. That looks nasty is it on your tummy too?"

I shook my head, pushing my dress back down over my legs. I knew I had a rash, the strange mottling was all over my body, but I had no intention of letting him see it. He seemed to take the hint. "Well I've got things to do if you want to be like that. I'll be back to check on you later." He left the room and - for an unknown reason - I was too afraid to take off the sun glasses. Not because I might go blind, but because of him.

I couldn't understand what was wrong with him. I sensed he was only pretending to be concerned, but why? My mum wasn't there to be impressed, and I certainly wasn't going to return home singing his praises. Why did he have to look at my rash? What difference would it make?

I watched the television, and the rest of the room became black. My hearing made up for my loss of vision, and I became conscious of strange noises behind me. I ignored them for a while, but my curiosity won and I sat upright looking to where the noises seemed to be coming from. The hall door was behind the couch. I peered over the back of the couch to see bright daylight in the crack of the door and something moving, obscuring the light to flashes. "What are you doing?" I called out.

"I'm polishing. Aren't you asleep yet?" He came back into the room, and a little light followed him. I didn't say a word. He sat on the floor next to the couch and pushed me back down on the couch. I could only see his shoulders and his head, and his left arm that was lifting my skirt again. He was shaking his head and looking very concerned. "You know I might have to take you to the hospital if your temperature doesn't drop soon." His hand was on my knee and began to slide a little higher. I froze and then panicked. I couldn't breathe in. The air in the room went solid and wouldn't fill my lungs - everything was silent. I had to break it or die. I sat up quickly, but with no idea what I was going to do next. For some reason, I must have frightened him because he jumped up and ran out of the room. He said he'd heard a knock at the door. I hadn't heard a knock.

    I looked at my legs in the dim light of the television. They did have a funny, jigsaw type pattern rash on them. I was a bit hot and tired, but there was no way I was going to fall asleep in the Gingerbread man's house. I was confused by the strange man who acted like no one I had ever encountered in my life. When he came back into the room a little later I pretended to be asleep. I didn't want to speak to him. I didn't want to see him. I just wished that the time would go faster and my mum would come and get me out of there. I would tell her how horrid it had been and she would never send me round there again. Even better she might never see Richard ever again, or take me to the Gingerbread meetings. It seemed simple in my immature head.

    To my relief, he switched off the television and left the room. I could hear him behind me again, behind the hall door. The noises I could hear didn't register as anything that I recognised, especially polishing. I couldn't smell polish at all. I opened my eyes slightly as my brain tried to figure out what was going on. The room was dim, but my eyes were adjusted and some light was shining in from the ajar hallway door. I could see a reflection of him in the television set. He was standing behind the door watching me. I closed my eyes tight again and vowed I wouldn't open them until my mum came to pick me up.

Finally, after the longest day of my life, so far, the doorbell rang. He opened it and my mum asked, "How's she been?"

"She's been asleep most of the day, so she wasn't too much trouble," he replied stressing the too. I hated him from that moment. I hadn't been any trouble. I never was. My mum wanted to carry me to the car. Richard offered to. I stood up and said, "I can walk. I haven't got polio or something." Richard frowned at the way I'd spoken, and my mum looked slightly embarrassed for my lack of gratitude, but I wasn't in the mood for 'Thank yous'.

I got into her silly little yellow bug car and she asked, "Do you like Richard?"

I waited until we'd driven out of his street, and his house was out of sight before answering, "No, I don't like Richard. Don't ever take me there again. I won't go anyway if you try to. You'll have to leave me at home on my own. He kept checking on me and wanting to see my rash, and lifting my dress up, and going behind the door, and making strange noises that he called polishing, with polish that had ran out because I didn't hear it or smell it, but he kept on polishing."

My mum was driving, nodding and agreed that he probably was polishing. That was when I realised that my mother was either stupid, or that she never actually listened to me at all, either way, from that day onwards I was on my own.

Breaking Glass

Before I knew it - that man - Richard was in our house all the time. He was there when I got home from school, and he didn't go home at night time. He made my mum laugh, he made my little sister laugh and he took us all swimming a lot, an awful lot. His slippers appeared In the hallway, and he was so at home that he would fart loudly creating a stench that was beyond description, but would make anyone heave. His little son, Earl, tagged along with him though neither of them looked very happy about it. His son was a miserable little git, but he had a reason to be. His mum was dead, and I supposed that would be enough to make any child miserable. We had to be nice to Earl and not upset him. I'd thought that I wouldn't be that miserable if my mum died, but I would be if Richard was my dad. I felt sorry for the kid. Earl was only a baby really about four years younger than me. I liked him. He'd have really aggressive, screaming, raging tantrums that Richard couldn't control. He'd hurl his toys in temper so hard, that he'd smashed the windows on many occasions, and however much Richard tried to restrain him, the boy would not respond to him in the way Richard wanted. Earl's main response to his father was to throw poo from his bedroom window whenever Richard left the house. Disgusting as it may be, this always brought a smile to my face.

Richard would tell us that it was Earl's way of coping with the loss of his mother and that we shouldn't be frightened of him - he was a stupid boy and didn't realise his own strength. Richard assured us that he'd look after us, and he'd make sure that Earl wouldn't ever hurt us. I wasn't worried about the messed up kid; he was on my side and we were going to be friends. I could also use him to make Richard look like a useless parent. It was very easy to get Earl into a tantrum state, and it was especially amusing in public. No, the kid was going to be fine with me. The only problem was his weird excuse of a father. Who calls their own kid 'stupid'?

Within a few months, Richard was there all the time. He had moved all his belongings in, including his little son. He became braver and more imaginative with his strange behaviour towards me - abusing my mind and my body. I was bewildered, and although he was always extremely careful not to leave any physical marks on my body, the long term mental damage was already beginning to take effect. I didn't understand anything that he did at the time. Sometimes I doubted myself and my own eyesight. It was all so unbelievably bizarre.

My mother took me to the doctor because I started blinking. She called it blinking, but it was more like closing my eyes tightly shut for two seconds then releasing them for five seconds then repeating this action over and over again. Sometimes a bout of blinking could last for over an hour. It annoyed everyone, especially Richard, so it was off to the doctor with me to get it fixed.

"She keeps blinking all the time," she said staring at me.

"How do you mean? Have you noticed if anything's wrong with her eye sight?" he questioned.

"Not as far as I know. She's had eye tests at school and they said she was fine. Look she does it all the time, but typical, she's not doing it now. Show him, show him what it's like." She was still staring at me. Her annoyance was clear. I squeezed my eyes shut and demonstrated my ailment to the doctor.

"It looks like a tic, a nervous twitch and I'm sorry, but I can't give her any medication for it. Could she be anxious about something? Have there been any changes at home?" He was addressing my mum, though his eyes flicked between the two of us.

"Everything's fine at home." She was shaking her head.

"How about school?" He seemed to want an answer from me, but she continued. "That's fine too. She is always top of the class."

"All I can suggest for the time being is that you encourage her to do it. Telling her to stop it will only draw more attention to it and make it worse. If she hasn't grown out of it in a month's time, I'll see her again." That was that. I hadn't gotten to say a word.

I know she was only taking the doctor's advice, but having two adults and two younger children all shouting at me to do it again and to do it faster while I couldn't control it at all, only ridiculed and humiliated me more. I did finally grow out of it, apparently. I rather think that when I discovered the magic swirls on the hallway carpet was when I no longer needed to do the blinking.

The carpet ran across the small landing, down the stairs and through the hallway from the kitchen to the front door. It was bright orange and dark brown in swirling, circling patterns. Every couple of feet the swirls turned into tight circles. I came down the stairs one day only stepping in the middle of the circles. I went through to the kitchen for my breakfast in the same way hopping from one to another. Then I left for school walking down the narrow hallway only in the middle of the circles. When I returned home after a good day at school, everything was quite normal and Richard didn't hurt me, or taunt me, or touch me in any way that evening. That was it, in my mind the bright orange and dark brown swirls in the carpet were magic swirls and would change everything as long as I kept up the routine.

Trying to always walk only on the circles without anyone noticing was quite tricky. If Richard had seen me and guessed what I was doing, he'd have had the carpet ripped up and a plain one put in to replace it. Then I would be helpless against him again. Sometimes he still hurt me, even though I thought I had stood on all the right circles. I decided that there must be a correct order to step on them. I tried different orders every day. Some days I got the order right and nothing happened to me. Some days I would forget the order or maybe the order changed every day or every week. It was so hard and frustrating trying to get it right - thinking I had got the order right only to discover later that evening that I must have got it horribly wrong. I continued trying to get it right, every morning, until we moved out of that house and the carpet, to my dismay, was left behind.

With frustration and anger, I pour myself another large Vodka. I have just realised that the thoughts and my memories are irrelevant to the court yet again. I have branched off on a tangent, but it seems important for me to remember these experiences, just as important to me as the specific details will be to a court.

Maybe thinking about all the other stuff, that the court is not interested in, will help me to recall the important stuff, and maybe it might help me make more sense of my life. Poor Earl, I do feel so sorry for him. He has made statements too and although he hates Richard, as much as the rest of us, it is his real father and he shares the same genes. I wonder how he must be feeling. After all he is my brother. I wouldn't have had a brother if Richard hadn't come along. My thoughts are with Earl, and they take me back to when I first got a brother.

Time

What felt like a couple of years passed, though it could have been a few months, and it was my mum and Richard's wedding day. We had moved into a house in the town. It was one of those big, terraced houses with a cellar that you can see into from the street. The front door was on the street, a bay window jutted out into the path and there were lots of faraway rooms, fireplaces and spiders. It was dark and it was cold. There were no swirling carpets anywhere. I hated that house. I hated living with Richard, and I hated having to go home to that house every day. The worst thing was to see the cellar light on from the street and my mum's car not parked outside.

My brother Earl - I classed him as my brother by then - and my little sister, who was roughly the same age as him, probably felt the same dread when they came home from school as I did. They had each other though. They'd started at the same primary school at the same time and they stuck together. I was in a new middle school on my own, without even a friend.

Richard had developed an obsession with time; you could call it a clock fetish. I couldn't understand what his fascination with 'time' was. It was almost like it was his partner in crime. It was used as a reason to punish and control us. It was his ally in his mission to send us all berserk. I remember a day when it was pissing down with rain. I knew exactly how long it would take me to get home, whatever the weather, so that I wouldn't be late, or early. The rain was heavy and the roads were flooded and oily. I knew I wasn't late; I was bang on time. I turned my bike into our street; we lived seven doors up. I mounted the pavement at the alleyway entrance where the kerbs were dropped, pulled the brakes and swerved into the front of our house. Unfortunately the brakes were wet and had picked up oil from the roads. The bike didn't even slow down. It hit the bay window at full speed. My crotch hit the handlebar post and my face hit the window frame, luckily not breaking the window, and I dropped to the floor with my bike. I was in agony. I should have fainted and lain there like any normal person would have, but no, I had to get up and get through that door on time. Dizzy, doubled up, blood pouring from my nose and soaked to the skin, I pulled myself up to the door. I opened it and slid along the wall inside. How I managed it was partly for fear of being late, and also to not give Richard the pleasure of punishing me. I lent my bike against the wall in the hallway, closed the door and collapsed in a heap on the floor.

Above me, timing me and watching me was a clocking-in and clocking-out clock. It must have spent its working life in a big Victorian factory somewhere - probably a shoe factory if it was from around here. It must have been over a hundred years old. It was in a very big, rectangular, wooden case. Its face was in the top half and still told the time in Roman Numerals. There was a space in the bottom half where the tickets would have been stamped by a machine. It didn't have any guts, or should I say any mechanisms in it, that it needed for printing the clocking-in and clocking-out tickets - they were missing. Its presence was still overbearing.

The clock just watched me lying there with my nose bleeding. Within seconds the house erupted into chiming and donging from all directions. I relaxed, knowing that I wasn't late.

That hall clock was one of the one hundred and fifty one clocks, at that present time, that had inhabited the house with us. There was a huge pine grandfather clock that, at some point, had been dipped into acid or stripped to regain its wooden body. It had been painted pink originally; you could tell because all the knots in the wood were still pink. It was the evilest clock in the house. The one that would betray you every time you were late. It was Richard's only trusted friend. It stood in the corner next to his armchair. It looked over him and watched us. It always told him the truth - it always told him that I was late. It didn't matter what the other one hundred and fifty clocks in the house told him. I hated that fucking clock. I would ridicule it to myself because it used to be painted pink, and one day it might get painted pink again, and I hoped it would be me that did it. It deserved to be pink again.

Along with that boss clock, there'd been other clocks in the living room: smaller mantle clocks, bracket clocks, ugly square clocks, stupid novelty clocks, a clock that was a naked, metal, cherub type child with wings who held up a very heavy looking clock for an unknown reason (probably as a punishment for getting home late). Throughout the house there were drawers full of old watches and pocket watches, even the time display on the video player and the oven had their own place in the clock hall of fame in that evil clock house.

At the end of the long hallway, that ran from the front door and through to the kitchen door at the far end of the house, was the freakiest clock of the house. It hung right above the entrance to the kitchen and could easily have been read from the house across the road's own kitchen if you left all the doors open. It was just a clock face. It seemed about four foot high by four foot wide. It was square in shape and so big that you could watch its hands moving. It had regular numbers and was made of plastic. It must have come out of a railway station or an airport because of the size of it. It was imposing on that journey along to the kitchen, actually seeing the time passing by. More than that though, it was scary - it had no body and it had no frame. I wondered how something could still work without a body - was it supernatural? If you'd smashed its face in, it would be gone. There was nothing else to it just that big square face.

I think that Richard actually chose that particular street to live in because the house at the entrance to our street had a giant sun dial on its side wall. It faced south into our street. It was the first thing you saw when turning into that street. It was never sunny enough to read it. It just reminded me to check the time; you might be late then you're going to get it, and if you're not late you're going to get it anyway. It was an irritating reminder. I always thought, 'One day, when I grow up, I'm going to buy that big stone house, and I'm going to paint shadow lines all over that fucking sun dial, so no one bothers looking at it anymore.'

I got a watch for Christmas that year. Surprise, surprise. Everyone at school had wanted a digital watch. It was a new fad, as my mother called it. Everyone wanted one except me, and I got one. I even had to go to town, to a watch shop, with Richard and pick the watch that he insisted he was going to buy me because that was what I wanted. I picked one that played *'Scotland the Brave'*. I really didn't like the idea of wearing the time with me, so I set it to the wrong time. I pretended I didn't know how to work it, and I decided that I was going to be as brave as Scotland one day, however brave that was. I annoyed everyone with that tune. It went off in school lessons, at dinner time, while Richard was watching the television and whenever I wanted to annoy someone.

I stop myself. I'm getting a bit drunk I fear,

and I'm not remembering anything significant. Sober, I get reminded constantly; every time I hear that name. It is a common name, it is one reason I don't watch the television. There are so many people on the television called Richard. There are so many programs about paedophiles. There are stories on the news and in the newspapers. I can go into a pub and the conversation at the bar will be about some paedophile. The usual comment is - "I can't understand why the kid never said anything at the time." Strangely I know and understand why nobody says anything at the time. That is all part of what paedophiles do. They didn't just fuck children; there is a whole manipulation process involved. I steer clear of those conversations. It would be such a long and complicated story; far too long for the attention of drunk guys at a bar. They also like to be right about everything, so I just let them not understand.

Maybe the actual events will come to me later - when they need to. Maybe they aren't important at this moment. They will be important to the court though. I'll ponder whatever comes into my head and drown myself in another vodka, as another memory fills my spinning head like a dream.

Five Years

I had been out; I'd been out somewhere that I shouldn't have been. So fucking what, I was eleven years old and the angriest kid on the block, and I was a liar, apparently, and everybody knew it.

I could have told the truth, but Richard would have made me out to be a liar. That's how it worked. He'd make everything I said or did into a lie. The few friends and relatives that we had were convinced that I was a liar and I couldn't be trusted. I was as much a liar as Earl was stupid. I saw how Richard did it to the both of us. He thought he was clever. I thought 'For now maybe, for now I have no voice, only for now.' For then, he was the grown up. I was just a lying, little glue-sniffing slag, and he made sure that everybody knew it. Amazingly, I'd never heard of glue-sniffing at that time, and I'd never had sex with anyone, willingly.

I had, when I was younger, always told the truth. I had no reason to lie to my mum. Even when Richard came along, I still told the truth because I still had no reason to lie, and I was also too scared of him. My telling the truth, but being branded a liar by the bastard, really pissed me off. Before, I didn't understand where he was coming from or what his intentions were, but then at around eleven years old, it was piecing itself together. Now I could tell you exactly what his intentions had been. All I knew then though, was that it was too late to tell anybody. I couldn't tell anybody what he was doing to me because nobody would ever believe me. I knew what his reaction and response to me would be, in any situation that I could put him in. I would always be the loser. I always turned out the baddie and everyone felt sorry for my mum. They thought Richard was so patient and my mum was so lucky to have him and his support at my 'difficult time'.

I was so angry the day that he said to me, in front of my mum, brother and sister, "So, where did you go today?"

"I went to school." My brain raced as I tried to figure out what game he was playing.

"Well, I expected nothing more than a lie from you. Try again because I know exactly where you've been." His eyes bored into my face. I could see the rest of the family's eyes; they were boring into me too, but not in the same way as Richard's. Their eyes were pleading with me. Willing me to spit out the truth. To get it over with and not make him angry. I wouldn't be the only one that would get his wrath.

I was confused, but it soon struck me what he was playing at. I burned with anger as a realised he had me in a catch twenty two. I knew I'd been to school and nowhere else. I had a horrible choice to make. I could stick to telling the truth and ignite the fuse, or I could give him what he wanted them all to hear and cripple my persona further.

"Well, do you want to drag this out all night?" he yelled.

My sister's face contorted, and I knew she was about to cry. I forced myself not to disagree with him and muttered with guilt, "Sorry, no I didn't go to school." I didn't feel guilty though. I was angry and I hated him so much that I wished him dead. I repeated over and over in my head, 'Just drop down dead,' while he continued an onslaught of insults at me, as I bounced between the walls in the hallway.

He'd won that round of the game that he'd invented. The game that I was only just learning the rules. I would never win because he set up the starting positions, and I knew I'd lost before I could make my first move.

I wanted to be bigger than him. One day I would be bigger than him, we all would and he knew it. That was why he was trying to fuck with our heads and brand me a liar. The relief on the others' faces was worth the giant extra chunk of hatred that I would carry with me for that man. And if he thought that he could ruin me or wreck me or kill me, he had one hell of an angry opponent.

I thought I was being strong at eleven years old. I really thought I could put up with all the abuse. I'd tell myself, 'only another five years and I'll be old enough to look after myself'. I didn't have a clue how much worse it was going to get and how constant mind games would wear me out.

The mental abuse that he was inflicting upon me was meant to drive me to suicide. That way he would be rid of the threat of me ever talking. I wasn't about to make his day though. He was worried that I hadn't even attempted to commit suicide. He'd say, "I don't know how you can live with yourself being nothing but a scrag end." He must have been getting frightened that I was getting to an age - and into some states - that I might just let it all out, even though I had it instilled in my head that I would never ever be believed. He knew that I probably would be believed if I spoke out, and he was afraid. That's why he tried to kill me.

Blackout

I had a red racing bike; it was my only friend. I loved that bike more than anything in the world. It was my only means of transport bar walking. It gave me time, time that I wouldn't have otherwise had.

The first injury sustained by my bike was minor. The gears locked up in the highest gear. I didn't know how to fix them. It was probably quite simple, but I didn't want to make them any worse. My bike was still rideable, and if I'd tinkered with it, I could end up losing it altogether. So I rode it how it was. This meant that I would either build my leg muscles up to the size of the Incredible Hulk's or I'd have to push the bike up the worst hills, then I'd be late home and then we'd all get his rage and, as usual, it would be all my fault. I wasn't going to be beaten - my leg muscles built up to be bigger than the Incredible Hulk's legs. My bike stayed in the highest gear until the day that Richard stole it.

Prior to him stealing it, he sabotaged my brakes. They didn't just break and stop working on slowing down. That would have been unmemorable.

When it happened was when I needed them the most; when I needed to pull them tight and fast.

I was riding down a really steep hill which had no traffic on it what so ever. A quiet street, because it went nowhere in one direction. It wasn't used unless you actually lived in the street. I had cut through a walkway at the top of the street. It was brilliant for flying down at top speed.

There were houses on both sides of the street. At the bottom of the hill was a T-junction. My view was blocked by the houses either side of the junction, but I had plenty of time to stop. The T-junction road was a busy main road. To go left was a 'slow down' then sharp turn and back up hill. To go right was a definite stop, wait for ages, then when it was clear pull out, turn right and carry on down the hill over a bridge spanning a lake. I had ridden that way hundreds of times.

I hurtled down the hill, and at the precise point I reached for the left brake lever and squeezed it; no harder than usual for the speed I was going. The whole thing came off in my hand. I quickly grabbed for the right lever and squeezed it hard, but more cautiously; I didn't fancy a trip over the handlebars. It also came off in my hand. I let go of it, and it dragged across the tarmac still connected to the cable and the wheel. I still had the left brake squashed in my hand that was gripped to the handle bars. I took the brake lever and crushed it against my thigh. I tried desperately to make some pressure to close the brakes. Nothing. I was going too fast to put my feet down, and it wouldn't have made any difference to my speed. I was at the junction before I could think. I stared down at the front wheel and the road beneath it. All I could do was steer. I didn't look left or right - there was no point. If I was going to get smashed into a million little pieces, I really didn't want to see it coming. Horns beeped but I was oblivious to everything around me.

Halfway down the hill towards the bridge, I realised that I had made it. I was stunned beyond belief. I hadn't been hit by any vehicle, even though the road was really busy. There were cars and lorries passing me on both sides of the road, and my brake was bouncing around my back wheel attached to the cable. I was so lucky, although a small part of me had accepted the worst, and it would have been an easy way out of my misery. I still couldn't stop or even slow down, but once over the bridge and the lakes, it was uphill again and my bike eventually slowed and stopped of its own accord. I decided that I wasn't just lucky at that moment, but that I had just won one of his games, and a battle with myself - Richard's attempt to destroy me, and against my own looming self-destruction.

I won't be able to mention my sabotaged bike in the court. Nor about how I survived that awful ride. There is no proof. No proof that he took all the screws out of my brakes to make me crash and die. I knew it was him though; it wasn't the only time that strange things happened that I couldn't prove. He may have induced me to be paranoid all of the time, but I knew it was him, and it was clear he wanted me dead. The court want me to remember and recall the proper criminal charges. They want me to tell them what he did to me that evening and all because I got home late, as I had to walk. He must have been so angry when I walked through that front door alive. So angry because he was waiting for a phone call to say that I had been splattered all across a road somewhere.

I remember how angry he was, and exactly what he did to me that night. It won't be difficult to recall. It is all in my memory like it had happened an hour ago, as easy to remember as that bike ride. It's just much harder to think about. I recalled everything in detail in my interviews. For some reason these other incidents and events seem far more important to me right now. They're at the front of my mind while the thoughts of the details that will emerge in court are pushed far away to the back.

I pour myself everything that is left in the Vodka bottle and recall the morning's phone conversation over and over. I wonder what Richard must be thinking, locked up in a cell. I wonder if Earl has heard the news. The room around me is strangely blurry, and my eyes are struggling to focus on anything. I squint and lean back on my chair, abruptly realising that I'm sitting on a stool. A whirl of ceiling and lampshade retreat from my vision. A thud and all is black. Nothing exists except the inside of my mind. A scorching flash shoots through my head, stars and pulsing lights whizz towards me and then out of view. I am nowhere, but everywhere and utterly bewildered.

Part 2 – Changes 1981.

Friday.

It's my fourteenth birthday; I was given a green mod parka, as a present this morning, which I have proudly worn to school today. I did want it, but I always hate getting clothes for my birthday - it's like getting food. Shouldn't your parents buy you clothes and food anyway?

I also received a couple of cards containing record vouchers, and I'm hoping to be let into town to spend them. My best present is an LP *'Scary monsters and super creeps'* that Richard bought me. He probably thinks that I'll take it as some kind of threat, but I really wanted it. I find it quite funny that the older I get the more pathetic Richard seems. I live in fear of my life and I struggle to play his game to my advantage, but he's taught me his tactics, and over time I've learnt how to manoeuvre and cheat.

Even though I'm not late home, I shudder and a lump presses hard in my throat, as I pull into the street. My mum's car isn't here. I swallow my insides back down, as I stand outside the house. The cellar light dimly glows out onto the pavement. I take a deep breath and the warmth that I'd built up cycling leaves my body, as it goes dead and cold. As I step onto the doorstep, I curl up into an imaginary ball and roll myself back into the furthest corner at the back of my head.

My hand turns the door knob and the door opens.

My feet and legs move involuntarily, pushing me and my bike over the threshold and the thick bristle mat into the hallway.

My hand pushes the door shut behind me, click.

My arms lean my bike against the hallway wall under the clocking-in and out clock.

My eyes glance at the clock. I am on time. It tells me that it is three forty precisely. It won't be so bad surely.

My feet step me forward to the lounge doorway.

My eyes glance down to my brother and sister sitting crossed legged on the floor in front of the television - their backs to Richard's empty armchair and the grandfather clock watching over them. Their eyes look up at me for a split of a second. No one says a word, and then their eyes go back to the television.

The hallway is silent. I walk as softly as I possibly can to the staircase. I want to run up it and hide, but that would only make things worse.

Footsteps come quietly nearer, as I watch the shadow grow bigger and higher against the giant clock with no body at the end of the dark hallway above the kitchen door.

A head appears around the top of the cellar stairs - it's Richard.

A nasally voice calls out, "Hey, nut rag, I need

you to hold something for me." He disappears back down into the cellar.

I feel all the senses of my body join me in my curled up place in the back of my head.

My legs walk to where I'm meant to go.

I stare straight ahead throughout the walk and the whole ordeal. I hate him so much. I want to be big. I want to burn his fucking eyes out of his fucking head, so he can no longer see me.

But I am a mere zombie; I do what I'm told. I say nothing unless I am asked. I stare into the distance as my sight goes blurry by the wetness that appears in my eyes at these times. I think it happens to stop me seeing, like the blinking used to when I was little. It can't be tears as I can feel nothing.

For the following half an hour or more, he works in the cellar singing songs of thrills and Blueberry hills in a cocky, happy voice. Everyone in the house seems to relax slightly now. They know there will be some peace for them for a while.

Me though, I can't wait to get out of this fucking hell house and go and get fucked some more, by nice, good people to dilute this fucking evil bastard. I'm not allowed out though because it's my birthday and I have to spend it with my family.

The rest of the evening I plan to work out an intricate percentage system. I have set out a graph and hide it in a box amongst my books. I can dilute the bastard to nothing, I'm sure of it. My mother enters my room.

"Being too old for birthday parties, we wondered what treat you'd like. Richard said that you wanted to see 'Friday the Thirteen', but I wasn't sure about it. You know it's a horror film don't you? Anyhow as it is your birthday, I agreed to let Richard take you. Try and make yourself look a bit older, else they might not let you in. Ok?" She leaves the room.

I am stunned and gutted. I've never said that I wanted to go and watch a horror film, and I don't want to go to the cinema with Richard. I know I can't argue it. I cover my face with my hands, but I'm not going to cry. He's not going to upset me or frighten me.

"*He can't kill you in a cinema, can he?*" My head seems to be talking to me, but it isn't my voice. I recognise it, but can't figure out where from. I get dressed up and ignore it. Maybe it was my head playing tricks, but it sounded so real.

I sit in the dark cinema taking no notice of the film or Richard. I count, in my head, the seconds and the minutes as they pass. Then it's all over. It was almost like I hadn't been there at all.

Back home I try to sleep. Richard probably won't be bothering me again tonight.

Saviour Machine
Saturday.

I wake up with my mission in mind. Maybe I'll be allowed out, maybe I won't. It's going to be a really long Saturday if not. It always depends on Richard's mood, and what he has planned for us in his sick head. If I am told that I am allowed out, then I will have to bolt. I won't be out until I am completely out of the street - out of earshot. I could have one foot out of the door, and he'll call me back to tell me that he's changed his mind. Then he'll grin and I'll know why, and I'll go to the place in the back of my head to take me away from my body; to switch myself off so that I don't go wild and crazy and get stuck like it forever if the wind changes.

Strangely, he decides that we've all been good this week and he gives us all a pound. "Get some chips and an ice-cream at the park, you've all earned it this week. I need to speak to your mother, so you needn't be home until seven," he says, in front of my mother of course.

Wow. I don't have to be home until seven o'clock.

Confusion presses against my temples. This evil bastard bloke thought he had it all going his way, but this kid has got him sussed. So he thinks that he's confused the situation, he thinks it will dwell on my mind that he is up to something and that I'll be frightened and go slightly madder.

Like I give a fuck. He is up to something and it isn't going to be nice. I will be blamed for doing terrible things today, I'm sure. All so he can punish us all, and then punish me more. It will be my fault and everyone will blame me, and hate me, especially my mum. It is going to happen whatever I do, so fuck it. I'm allowed out and I'm not going to worry about it at all. I know exactly what I am going to do and why.

I'm out of the street in a blink of an eye.

"Where are we going Marie?" Damn that weird voice isn't coming with me. This time I answer it in my head. 'Well, I'm going to my friend Tex's house and you aren't coming with me.'

"Who's Tex?" It continues.

'If I tell you will you go away?'

"Maybe."

'Promise me or I won't tell you.'

"I'll find out anyway, shortly enough."

'Don't play games with me. I've been taught well.'

"Okay, I promise to go away if you tell me."

I stop at the corner of Tex's street.

'Tex is a guy that I spoke to in a shop once when I was a few pence short for something. He gave me the change that I needed and tried to make conversation with me. I was polite, but embarrassed. After that, every time I saw him around, he'd make a point to say hello until one day, I was in a right bad state. I was very upset about something. He's a bit older than me, probably seventeen, but he doesn't know how old I am. He lives in the flat above that hairdressers' shop with his flat mate, Al, who is hardly ever there. He must have been concerned about me when I met him that day. He took me to his flat and gave me a glass of coke and tried in vain to find out what was wrong with me. I just kept repeating, over and over, for him to stop asking me 'what the matter was'. He found that amusing - the way I phrased it - and he kept laughing. I'm sure he was genuinely concerned. He told me where I could find the door key to his flat. If I ever needed somewhere to go, I could go there even if there was no one home. The door to the flat is downstairs so's the kitchen. The rest of the rooms, living room and bedrooms are upstairs above the hairdressers' shop. The whole place smells clean - of shampoo. That's it.'

"So you go there because it smells clean?"

'No, don't be dumb. I was grateful of the invitation. I quite often spend my time riding around - going nowhere as I have nowhere to go - rather than going home. It is really horrid when it's raining or snowing, but not half as horrid as it is at home. Anyhow, I took up the offer and go there whenever I get the chance. I let myself into Tex's flat two or three times a week. If no one's home I do the washing up, clean the kitchen and vacuum the place up. It passes the time and it makes me happy. It is like my pretend grown up home. I can forget where I really live, for a while. He hugs me and thanks me for cleaning the kitchen, and he tells me that I don't have to do it. What he doesn't realise is that I don't actually do it to please him. I'm just glad to be out of that fucking hellhole that I live in. If I sit in front of his television he might think that I'm taking the piss. He might get fed up and move the keys. Whereas, if I do something useful like cleaning the kitchen, he'll put up with me. I'm lucky. Not many people would put up with a fucked up, lying, glue-sniffing, little slag in their house.'

"Oh, you shouldn't talk about yourself like that Marie. What will people think?"

'They'll think what they already think; what Richard has made them believe.' I huff as a woman comes towards me. She crosses the road and looks over at me. 'Can you please go now? I'm getting some strange looks just standing here.'

"I'm not sure I should. What if something happens to you?"

"Ha," I speak out loud and bite my tongue. 'It's a bit late to worry about that. I was at Tex's recently and he came in drunk - it was inevitable really. I grabbed him as usual to greet him. He hugged me back, and told me that I was the weirdest and most beautiful girl that he'd ever met. I gripped on to him so tight that he couldn't unhug me. He carried me up the stairs and into his bedroom and fucked me - in a nice, loving way - in a drunken way. It didn't matter though. I can't say I didn't like it and I can't say that I did, but I realised that I had diluted Richard. The strength of the overpowering control - that rushed through my veins - was so great that I would have let anyone and anything fuck me - just to dilute Richard a little bit more. It is so utterly empowering, and I don't care about my body anyway - it isn't part of me anymore. I can detach myself from it and hide in a small place in my head when Richard bothers me. My body is poisoned, but I've discovered a way of diluting the poison. I feel a little bit better about myself, so please leave me alone now. I really don't have time for this.'

"I'm sorry, I'll leave you to it."

'Bye.'

The front door isn't locked, so I know Tex is at home. Walking straight in, I grab him and wrap myself around him without even speaking to him. I close my eyes and nuzzle my head under his rough chin.

"You really should knock. My parents or someone might have been here."

"I'm sorry. I'm in a rush."

"You're always in a rush. Come on then my little Russian doll."

He lifts be up, carries me to his bedroom, throws me onto his bed, undresses me and fucks me.

Afterwards - looking content with his arm around me - he goes to say something, but I jump up - I haven't got time for listening to any bullshit.

"Sorry, I have to go." I throw on my clothes.

He looks slightly bewildered, but doesn't really give a fuck. He's had what he wanted. I am on a diluting Richard spree, and nothing is going to slow me down - let alone stop me.

Dragging my battered bike out of the hallway, I slam the door behind me. The brakes are screwed back on, and I bandaged them with tape to stop Richard getting to them again. I'm still stuck in the highest gear, but it makes me go faster, and my legs are getting stronger.

I head for the park. It's a great park - it's my park. It has three lakes all connected by little streams and bridges, lots of little spinneys, a massive kiddies' play area, a church with a graveyard full of grave stones - hundreds of years old, a museum that's been closed for years, a golf course, rugby pitches, goal posts, a real old fashioned band stand, ice cream vans, tame squirrels, a folly that is home to a million pigeons and doves, hissing swans that can break your arm and ducks and peacocks that just wander around. It's a fantastic park. Well it is if you're me, or a little kid, or a fisherman.

I ride down to the big fishing lake - slowing down - circling it. There are quite a few people fishing. One guy looks about my age and quite nice. I stop next to him. "Have you caught anything?"

He looks at me from of the corner of his eye, his face starts to go red, then he makes a murmuring grunt and shakes his head. I will take that as a no.

A little further along is a quite handsome dark haired guy. He's older than me, probably the same age as Tex, so when I get to him I ask him the same.

He gives me a beaming smile with sparklingly white teeth and points to his keep net.

I take this as an invitation to sit down next to him, as I can't see what's in his net from up here. I rest my bike down behind him and join him on the ledge peering over the edge looking for the fish.

"It's a chub - probably weighs about ten pounds." Pride is written all over his face. It doesn't look that big to me, but I'm not really interested in the fish, so I nod and try to look impressed. Then he holds out the rod to me. I take it, and surprise, surprise, he wraps his arms around me to show me how to hold the bloody thing (like I've never been fishing) and how to hook the fish gently instead of firing it into the trees behind, like most girls do when they get a bite. He tries making conversation, so I kiss him. I don't have time to talk. He kisses me back. I pull at him to get up, and we walk into the bushes. He fucks me against a rotten tree. While he's doing it, I notice some coins falling out of the pockets of his trousers into the leaves and bark surrounding this rotting tree. When he's finished he smiles shaking his head in disbelief, "What's your name?"

I'm pulling up my trousers while rifling the undergrowth for the coins that he spilt. I don't answer. I just kiss him and say, "Bye." I rush out from the bush, jump on my bike and ride off.

I stop at the litter bin at the duck feeding end of the lake. There are always bread bags in the bins here left by the people who feed the ducks.

I stuff three into my pocket and ride out of the park - as fast as I can - towards the shop that sells glue. It would be impossible on foot. It would take three quarters of an hour at least, but the local shops won't sell glue and they're too close to home to risk it. It hardly takes me five minutes to get to the shop on my bike.

With the pound that Richard gave me and the change that the fisherman dropped, I have enough money to buy two tubes of glue.

I go into the shop accompanied by my bike. "Two tubes of Evo-Stik please." I have to ask the shopkeeper for the glue, as it's behind the counter. I think it gets nicked if it's left on the shelves. I buy it here regularly, as lots of the kids don't look old enough to buy it. Those that do, the shop keeper won't serve because their dads have been into his shop and threatened to kill him. He always serves me though, so the other kids ask me to get it for them and they let me have a bit.

"Wad do you wandit for?" he asks me.

"I'm building an aeroplane." I always say this, then he always sells it to me. I don't know why he asks me anymore. One day he might ask if I'm building a jumbo jet - I would - as it must be a big aeroplane due to the amount of glue that's needed. I get served the glue and leave the shop.

On my way out he shouts something to me. I stick my thumb up to him. I know what he said, "Next time, leave your bluddy bike outside." He says it every time.

It's starting to spit with rain and the sky is very dark. It's going to thunder - I have a knack of sensing things like this.

I would have gone back to the park, but I'll get drenched through. The Children's Home is nearer.

"And what's there?"

'I thought you promised to go away.'

"I did. Now I'm back. You're not busy - just wandering. Tell me why we're going to the Home?"

'Because, the Children's Home is where the only kind of friend that I have made recently - ever - lives. There's an alley behind the Home and a disused garage with a broken door that the kids from the Home use to glue sniff in when it's raining, or just to hide in if they want to be left alone. I try to avoid using it out of selfishness really. There are about ten kids live in the Home at any one time, and if you're the only one with glue, they expect you to share it. I don't mind today as I have two tubes.'

That seems to have satisfied that damn voice, but I wonder whether the voice might also speak to Richard. I should be more careful what I tell it from now on.

I reach the alley as the heavens open. It's cobbled with small, square, grey cobbles. They are very old, some have sunk and some jut up like rocks. In places, the worse holes have been concreted over, others have sunk out of sight just to be left to fill with water. There are puddles everywhere, and some will be really deep. I get off my bike and push it. I don't want to wreck the rims. I need my bike too much.

It's well worth getting soaked to save it. It's my companion, it's my escape, and it's the only thing that should be between my legs at my age.

I wonder if Doris will be at the garage.

"*Who's Doris?*"

I hesitate to answer.

'You won't repeat any of what I tell you, will you? '

"*How can I? I'm in your head.*"

'Not always.'

"*I promise not to go in anyone else's head and repeat anything you say.*"

'Okay. Doris is a kind of friend I have, and the reason I've got to know all of these other kids. She is the same age as me, although the only other people I know called Doris are really old, like someone's Nan.'

"*So why did you choose Doris?*" it continues.

The voice is kind of annoying me, but I feel the need to answer it. I don't want it to go away and leave me on my own.

'I didn't choose to befriend Doris - she chose me. She goes to my school, and that is the only thing that we have in common. She isn't in any of my classes, and I don't know any of her friends. She appeared in the dinner queue beside me a few weeks ago. I was standing about halfway down, and it's a pretty long queue because most of the kids in the school get free school dinners. All of our parents are unemployed, or on training courses of some description, so it's always a long wait. If we were given money instead, the majority of the kids wouldn't stand in the queue at all. The money would be spent on cigarettes, or at the chip shop. Anyhow, Doris came up to me in the queue and she just stood there, grinning with a great big, mad smile on her face. I ignored her at first. Then she nudged me pretty hard and asked me what my fucking name was. I frowned at her and didn't answer at first, but I took a good look at the little smart arse just in case I came across her again. I gave her a bad stare hoping she'd feel uncomfortable and fuck off away from me. She didn't budge and started to speak to me. She told me that she thought she'd stand with me because I looked like the most miserable and hardest girl in the queue, and nobody would say anything about her pushing in if she was with me. She had a cheek about her that I liked. I couldn't help but smile and I told her my name. That is all I've ever told her though. I've seen her every day at school since, or I visit her at the Home. I've never told her anything about my life. How can I complain to children that have lost their families or been through hell that I'm not happy in an apparently perfect home?'

"Did Doris tell you about her life?"

'She doesn't say much at all. We just watch telly, but she did tell me why she's in the home. You see, her mum was mad and used to hit her around the head with anything that was to hand. She'd been reported after she'd chased Doris down the street with a hot frying pan - still with sausages in it. She'd caught Doris and stood bashing her over the head with the pan in front of all the neighbours while dogs snatched the flying sausages. It sounded too much like Punch and Judy to be real, but that is what she told me happened, and I have no reason not to believe her. Then Doris kept getting into fights because she was angry with other kids. They picked on her mum and called her Dozy Rosey. Doris always sticks up for her mum, even though the woman had beaten her and made her life hell. That's why she is in care.'

"What do your parents think of Doris?"

'Don't call them my parents. You mean my mum and her husband, Richard.'

"Point taken - an easy mistake. You are very touchy aren't you?"

'Wouldn't you be? Listen, when I told my mum and Richard about Doris and the children's home, they were pleased that I had a friend and allowed me to visit. I heard Richard say to my mum, "Well at least we know that she'll be supervised at all times." More like he's letting me mix with - what he'll call - a bad crowd and I have become a bit more of a problem child. I don't care what his reasons are - I have fun there. The place is so big that you can disappear in it for hours, and the staffs' shift system means that they don't know who is in or who is out most of the time. Last week I convinced one stand-in member of staff - who had never met any of us before - that my name was Fiona and that I lived there. She must have looked so stupid reporting me missing that night.'

"You found that amusing?"

'Yes of course I did. Haven't you noticed that I'm on a mission to piss off adults?' There is no reply, so I carry on explaining and pushing my bike. I can't get any wetter than I already am.

'I've met three boys there too, all glue-sniffers. Pat is the oldest, sixteen. He's a skinhead, has a number one haircut, skinny legs squeezed into tight patchy bleached jeans, bony elbows, red braces and Doctor Martin boots that reach his knees with laces that must be a mile long. He told me his family had come from Ireland. His dad had got into a lot of trouble over there and his mum brought Pat over here. Something bad happened to his mum which he didn't explain. She died anyhow and he's been in care and foster homes ever since. He doesn't seem to remember a lot, or maybe he doesn't want to. He is very happy in the home, but he has to leave soon. He'd been to a school for naughty kids, so he must have done something wrong, but now he's on a YTS. He's always nice to me and everyone else - including the social workers and his probation officer.' I have almost reached the garage, but not finished my story, so I pause for a break.

'Dan does talk about his mum, and always when he is high on glue. I'm normally high too, so I've forgotten what he told me. It must be because he misses her. He remembers the good times that he had with her. I think the social services took him because she was an unfit mother and didn't, or wasn't able to take care of him properly. He's got an original mod parka, unlike my new, crappy copy. He's a smart haircut, but he has chubby, rosy-red cheeks. Hopefully he'll grow out of that when he's older. He makes model aeroplanes. In fact it was Dan who told me to tell the man in the glue shop that I'm building an aeroplane. He's pretty clever in a cute, crafty way. He always gets himself out of trouble, sometimes just by grinning with those fat rosy cheeks. And then there's Pete, now he doesn't talk to me or anyone about anything. He walks around on tiptoes even with shoes on. He has to have injections in his arm for some illness, no one knows why. He's always the smartest of the three dress-wise. He's got a real mod parka too, but usually wears a striped blue and white blazer. He tiptoes around in the cleanest, red, white and blue bowling shoes that I've ever seen. He always smells clean, and his hair is always immaculately styled and shiny. I don't know why he's in the home. He is extremely polite and well mannered. I don't think he's from round here. He just isn't a very talkative person, but then neither am I.'

"*Really, you don't like talking?*"

'Don't be sarcastic. You should think yourself privileged. I don't talk to anyone usually.'

"*I'll take that on board. It sounds like a big Home for only four kids.*"

'There are other children that live in the home. Many are younger and I don't know them. Others are there short term - sometimes only a week or so. I only know them three and Doris.'

"*And what are we up to now then?*"

'Who are you? Everything is a question with you, but you never answer any of mine. You better not be a grown up. I've told you I'm on a mission to piss off all grownups. I'm trying to not do what Richard expects, and to confuse him as much as he tries to confuse me, so you better not tell him anything. I know letting people fuck me is wrong, but it puts me in control. It's only diluting the badness, after all. Go away now, if there's anybody in here, they'll think I'm mad.'

"*Aren't you?*"

'Fuck off will you.'

I push open the green, wooden garage door, wheel in my bike and rest it against the wet wall. I pull the door to, but it never closes completely. Four boys are sitting in a row along the opposite wall in the driest part of the garage. I recognise the three from the Home, but the fourth boy I have never seen before - he might be a new kid.

Pat stares with glazed eyes straight towards me.

"Hi Pat." I give a little wave, but he doesn't acknowledge my presence.

Beside him, Dan looks up and smiles. "You're in luck today. Pat has nicked the biggest pot of glue ever from his YTS job."

I hold up a tube and shrug my shoulders - at least I have mine to myself. I can't take it home with me anyway. Dan looks over to Pete and giggles. "I think he's found something," he says.

Pete is pointing at the ground, and following something slowly with his finger. It must be an ant or something imaginary because I can't see anything. He is really concentrating hard on it, his face is focused, fascinated and amazed. I don't say anything; I don't want to disturb him. His face is making me eager to get settled and get my bag filled.

The boy, who I don't know, waves at me as I cross the garage floor and sit down next to Pat. The new kid starts laughing and shouting out, "Look, Snow White has come to visit on a bike. Can you see her? It's Snow White, really it is. I'm gonna freak out when the dwarfs come in. Look will, ya?" He pulls at Pete and jabbingly points at me. He becomes quite hysterical. Pete stops looking at the fascinating floor creature and hits the boy around the face without even focusing on him, then he searches the floor again desperately - the creature must have vanished. The new boy stops laughing and pointing, but he checks every few minutes to see that I'm still here, and not a figment of his imagination.

I take out one of the bread bags that I got from the duck end bin in the park; *Sunblest* bags are always the best. They are soft and comfortable, quiet but strong; unlike some bread bags that are really 'plasticky' and crunchy and crinkly and noisy. I had picked two Sunblest bags from the bin - the other is a Co-op's own brand bread bag. That will do for emergencies, or if anyone else turns up without a bag.

I blow the bag up to its full capacity, hold it closed tight and squeeze it gently - wait for a few seconds - great, it hasn't got any holes in it. I tie a knot in the bag about halfway down. Now it's just the right size for my lung capacity - perfect. As I go to take the lid off of my tube, Pat nudges me in the ribs with his bony elbow. He shakes his head and hands me his big pot of glue that he is so proud of stealing from the YTS. It's the biggest pot of glue I've ever seen or held. I do have to get rid of the tubes before I go home, but the pot has a power of its own that the tube lacks. When you open a tube of glue you are not hit with its power like you are when you open a pot. A tube dribbles into the bag, and you can hardly smell the trickle. The pot however hits your senses the minute you open it. The smell is in your nose, throat, eyes, and all around you. You can see it all sitting in the pot like thick sweet honey. There's no rolling over and over the end of a tube - just pour into the bag a big greedy pool of honey. I'm relaxed and I haven't even started yet.

I take a generous, but not too greedy portion from Pat's giant glue pot and my bag is ready. I hold it up to my mouth to kiss it. I love it and I breathe it, and breathe it, and relax, and breathe it. I am warm. The world wraps around me and holds me safe. I forget, and I don't care about anything. The buzzing begins in my ears and takes away all the other noises around me. It takes away the rain banging on the roof and running down the opposite wall. It takes away the idiots that are sitting here with me in their own little glue fuelled worlds. It takes away my nightmare existence. Only buzzing. My eyes are shut, yet I can see. I can see that everything makes sense - the whole of everything that there ever has been is with me, and it will all turn out alright in the end. Then I hear David Bowie singing a song in my head. No one else can hear it - it has only been sent to my head.

Someone fucks me. I know it was one of the four here with me, but I'm unsure which one. It was probably Dan as he was the only one that looked unaffected by the glue when I arrived. Pat was closest to me though, so it could have been him. I wasn't actually taking notice. I don't care who it was. It was a dilutant. It makes me feel even better.

A loud bang catches my attention, and I open my eyes. The garage door has been blown wide open. I look out - it is pretty dark. It's early but the storm clouds have made it almost like night time.

The lightning flashes and shows the alley in bright daylight for a second. There is a river right outside the garage door. A huge, wide river that's raging strongly. I'm glad I'm not out there. I shudder and clench hold of Pat's bony elbow. Then I notice a huge grey crocodile laying right in the middle of the river; it's lying dead still watching something and stealthily waiting. I stretch my neck out to see further; to see what the crocodile is watching. To my disbelief there is a baby dressed in white on the opposite bank. It hasn't noticed that the crocodile is there, and is waiting for his chance to snatch it and eat it up. Fear and panic fill my world, but I have to do something. My heartbeat pounds strong in my chest - I am superhuman.

I let go of Pat's bony elbow, jump up and run out of the garage door. I leap the raging river in one enormous bound, almost defying gravity, and run along the bank on the other side. The crocodile still has its eyes fixed on the baby, but he hasn't noticed me yet. I reach the baby and grab it up into my arms. The crocodile is mad, and it turns to snap at me. I run back along the bank, leap across the river, burst back through the garage door and sit back down next to Pat. I'm sweating, shaking and my heart is pounding so hard that I'm sure it's going to explode out of my chest. I look at the baby. It's fine - thank God. I sit it down on the other side of me and carry on breathing my glue bag, and become invisible and non-existent.

My glue all dried up - I slip back to reality. The

dread returns to the pits of my stomach. The glue bag is on the floor - dry and useless, and with each breath of air I take in, I get a little more back to normal. I look around the garage. Pat and the strange kid, who I didn't know, are gone. Dan is now staring with his eyes all glazed over. Pete gets himself up, brushes himself down and stretches, as if he's just got up from a good night's sleep. "Bye," he says and tiptoes out of the garage. I look to the side of me for the baby I rescued, reaching out my arm to it. There is only a white carrier bag beside me; it's full of paper, cans and potato peelings. Although my watch is set to the wrong time, I know how wrong it is. I still have half an hour before I have to be home. I throw the two tubes of glue and the spare bread bags onto Dan's lap; they are no use to me now. He doesn't even flinch. He's away in his dream world.

Taking hold of my trusty bike, I leave the leaky haven and head down the alley. I walk around in the rain taking in air for twenty nine minutes, while the voice in my head tries to bother me. I ignore it. I have to prepare my mind, ready for whatever I'm to encounter when I get home. I hate the thought that my bike is getting wet and might go rusty, but I'm not going home even one minute early.

I arrive dead on time, and I'm ushered into the living room where Earl and my sister are sitting on the floor. I sit down next to them. Richard's nasally, self-important voice rings through even when he's trying to sound concerned. "I have some pretty unpleasant news that has only just come to my attention. A young girl was raped in the park yesterday evening, so I don't want any of you going there again. I wouldn't want anything like that happening to any of you. Your mother agrees that it's very dangerous, especially for you." His eyes focus like an eagle's on mine.

'The stupid bitch always agrees with you. Fucking drop down dead both of you,' is my only thought on the matter.

Sons of the Silent Age
Sunday.

I wake up and my first thought is, 'I hate fucking Sundays.'

"*What every Sunday?*" the voice questions.

'Yes, every Sunday. Sunday is Richard's day, if you hadn't noticed. How long have you been following me around?'

"*Never on a Sunday, so what's so bad?*"

'It is as ceremonious as going to church. Except that you don't spend an hour or so in God's company, you spent the whole fucking day in Richard world. On Sunday no one goes anywhere. My mum will spend the majority of the day cooking, and this evening Richard's brother and his wife will come around with their four kids for drinks and act like they are privileged to be invited. I think they want to be like my mum and Richard. I can't understand why, as they are the nicest and most normal family that I know. They must be mad to come here and drink with that man. He might fuck one of their kids when no one is looking. They don't see that side of him though. Richard is clever at changing from one character to another depending on the company, and to suit himself. Please stop asking me questions. I have to find things to do.'

Earl, my sister and I wander around the house finding jobs to do. I clean out the rabbit hutch, we tidy our rooms, catch up on homework and find anything that we can do to avoid attracting attention or looking lazy. Sadly there is no escape from hateful Sunday dinnertime. It's the one day in the week that I get to see my mother and my brother get more shit than me. Should I be grateful, no, it just makes me more hateful - it makes me want to kill the bastard even more, and I have to sit through it yet again.

On the way to the kitchen, I remind Earl how far the moon is from Earth. He gives me a small nod, but doesn't say a word.

We all get seated at the table - two o'clock precisely. It's a ridiculously big, rectangular dining table with big chairs. Earl is opposite me. I can just see his head and shoulders above the table. My sister, next to me can hardly see onto the table.

Richard is at the far end near the window and my mum will sit at the other end nearest the door once she's served the food. She's lucky, she's the furthest one from him.

I wait for the plate to be put in front of me. The plate lands; we have Brussels again. No one speaks except that bloody voice in my head, "*What's so bad about Brussels*?"

'We hate fucking Brussels. I hate the fucking things more than anyone. Richard knows that we hate fucking Brussels, and that's why we have them every fucking Sunday. I don't have a problem with greens. I'm not a fussy eater. I can deal with peas, cabbage, broccoli, beans, cauliflower even spinach, but I hate fucking Brussels because they smell exactly like Richard's testicles. Richard knows this and that's why he makes us stay at home on Sunday and eat fucking Brussels and sit at this stupid, ridiculous table with him sat at the end acting like the king and my mum acting like the servant.'

I become aware that my face is contorting with the conversation that I'm having in my head. 'Go away before you get me in trouble.'

I look over at Earl; he ignores me. I stretch to kick at his foot under the table, but I can't reach. He is doing the zombie thing that I do so well. He doesn't want to be here as much as I don't.

The dinner is all dished up and we all eat in silence. I swallow the Brussels virtually whole, so that I don't have to taste them. I could consume them all if I could hold my nose and close my eyes, but that would please Richard. He'll get a kick out of knowing just how bad I feel and then I'll get twice as many of the fucking horrid things next week. The rest of the dinner isn't too bad, it's edible, if you like burnt potatoes. I have to squash a very large Brussels sprout up into a burnt potato and mash it with gravy so I can't taste it so much; it is too big to swallow whole. My mum is getting anxious and giving me worried glances. She doesn't want me to mess with my food because it'll give Richard a reason to flip his lid. The thing is, he doesn't need a reason to flip; he is going to do it anyway and soon.

We finish our dinners. My little sister has

eaten all of her dinner and her Brussels. Earl has finished pushing his dinner around the plate and is looking like a glue-sniffer, all glazed over, even though I know he isn't.

We put our knives and forks together on our plates politely. One of us has to be the first to say, 'Please may I leave the table?' None of us want to be the one to say it, but all of us want to leave right now. We all know it's a pointless question to ask and we all know what the answer will be: 'Yes, but not yet.' One of us still has to say it or we will all sit like this forever.

I try again to kick Earl from under the table. I know what is coming and I want to help him. He won't look at me. He doesn't even blink. He just looks past me.

"You haven't finished your greens," the piece of shit on the throne at the end of the table says. I have tried to hide a couple of Brussels under the chicken bones and my knife and fork, but Richard has seen me.

I pick one up. "They're lovely, but I'm full," I try to explain. A scream of an unidentifiable word forces me to eat a Brussels. My mum and my sister jump, but Earl doesn't move; he has gone rigid.

I want to spit the nasty, rancid, sweaty ball Brussels, bastard thing into Richard's fucking face, but I can't - I would die. I don't have anywhere to go, so I could stay sitting here forever while he screams, but it would cause everyone more shit. The others look at me; willing me to eat. I know they won't be allowed to leave the table until I've finished. I eat the last, horrid, bastard Brussels. Not only does my stomach retch at swallowing the fucking ball, but my brain is flooded with images of Richard's filthy, sweaty balls which I seriously want to kick till they fly out of his fucking evil eyeballs.

My plate clear I ask the question, "Please may I get down?"

"Yes, but not yet," Is his predictable reply.

We all know what is coming now, and I can see the rage in Earl's eyes building up. Richard begins quick firing questions at us, geography, maths, science, history. The same questions are asked each week until we know the answers. Then more questions are added once we've learnt the answers. It doesn't matter how many answers we get right - there will always be another lot waiting that we probably don't know. I'm sure he does it to make Earl feel a bit more stupid.

My mum takes all of the plates away to wash up. She doesn't want to be here either by the way her hands are trembling. She is putting stuff in the rubbish and running the sink and I can read her mind. She is begging us not to upset Richard. She is praying that we get the answers right.

My little sister just sits, still and silent. She has learnt her own way of being as unnoticeable as possible.

Earl is red and angry already and he hasn't even been spoken to yet.

I just want to kill the bastard, Brussels loving

Richard for all our sakes. If I could get hold of some poison, I could get it into his Sunday dinner. We could all eat our dinner and watch Richard choke until he went blue and bleed from the inside out, then slump onto the table completely dead. We could eat what we wanted and leave the fucking Brussels. We could play a different game after dinner. I could pull his eyes out and replace them with fucking Brussels.

I answer as many of the questions as I can, one after another. I hope the younger ones are taking in the answers because he has a habit of repeating a question and aiming it at one of them to see if they were paying attention. I answer the questions to try to keep him calm, so that he doesn't flip and give everyone hell. He is going to give us hell anyway, but I have to try.

I am told not to answer any more questions. My sister starts to answer, then she is told not to answer anymore. The next question is just for Earl. We all know what one of the questions will be. It is the same question that Richard asks Earl every week, and he never answers it.

"How far away is the moon from the earth?" There is snidiness in his nasally voice.

I had told Earl the answer before dinner and he's heard the answer so many times before, week after week. I can't understand why he doesn't just say it. He has his own reasons I suppose. He doesn't speak, his eyes are filling with tears and his face is getting redder.

Richard just stares at Earl. Demanding with his eyes that he speaks - any answer will do whether it is right or wrong. Earl doesn't say a word.

Richard stands up and smacks his hands down on the table. He screams like a sergeant major, "You're not only an imbecile, but an insolent one at that you cretin." My mum clatters the plates in the sink and turns. "Please Richard is..."

Before she can finish, Richard picks up his chair and launches it across the room at her. She yelps as it hits her and falls to the floor. She turns back to the washing up.

. Earl still doesn't speak; he doesn't even look at Richard. He is just staring forward with his eyes fixed on something behind my head. Richard is thumping the table. Still screaming, he picks it up then crashes it back down. The salt pot bounces towards him. He grabs it up and throws it at Earl's head. It hits him hard and flies off into the hallway. Earl still doesn't move or say a word.

My sister is shaking and starts to cry. Earl keeps staring straight ahead. Richard is now squealing things that don't even sound like words and he marches out of the kitchen slamming the door. He goes through into the front room and slams that door too. We stay sat at the table; we haven't been told that we can leave yet.

Ten minutes of silence and Richard returns. He looks at us expectantly one at a time. "Please may I get down?" I ask.

"Yes, all go to your rooms," he squawks, standing tall like he's a soldier.

It's a relief to get out of the kitchen, but we know this is just an interlude.

My sister gets into her bed. She doesn't try to sleep - she's staring up at the ceiling. I sit on my bed and wait. Half an hour of peace passes and then the house is filled with a shrill whistling noise. It stops for a second or two, then again and again the urgent whistle sounds. I get up to investigate; this is a new one on me. I go out on to the landing. Earl is looking out of his bedroom door; he is still at boiling point.

Richard is standing at the bottom of the stairs blowing a PE teacher's whistle. I look back at Earl standing there in his pyjama trousers, a foot too short for his legs. I guess he'd decided to go to bed too.

Richard blows the whistle again and shouts in his sergeant's voice at us, "Attention. If it had been a real emergency you would all be dead by now."

Earl and I stand at the top of the stairs and my sister joins us. We wait.

"All of you get into your pyjamas and into bed. The next time you hear the whistle you have two minutes to be dressed in your school uniforms and standing at the bottom of the stairs before I blow the second whistle." He walks out of sight.

We don't speak to each other. We go back to our rooms. I change into my night clothes. I'm not even going to try to figure out why we have to do this. The best thing is to just get on with it. Hopefully then he'll leave us alone.

I start reading a book. My sister is again staring at the ceiling. The whistle blows. I jump out of bed and pull my sister out of hers. I get my uniform on pretty quick, but my sister can't find any socks. I grab a pair of mine and try to help her by pulling them on to her feet while she fumbles with her blouse buttons. The whistle blows again. None of us have made it out of our rooms, let alone to the bottom of the stairs.

"Useless imbeciles are dead! Get back to your beds," he screams.

Trying to make the task easier, I lay out our uniforms so that we can jump straight into them. I tie our ties, so we can put them over our heads and pull them tight. I hang our blazers on the back of the bedroom door, so that we'll be on our way out of the room while putting them on.

We lay waiting. I try to read, but I can't relax enough. I want to climb out of the window and run away. Looking up at the window, I notice something that wasn't there before. The window has screws along the middle frame where the locking catch is. They hadn't been there before. He has screwed my window closed; I am now a prisoner in this room. He is unbelievable. Maybe he is planning on doing such horrid things to me that he knows I will try to run away. He doesn't want me to run away though; he wants me to die, so I can never tell anyone what he is like.

Before I can investigate the window, our bedroom door opens and Richard comes in. We never hear Richard walking up the stairs. He must have worked out where all the creaky floor boards are. He just appears in the room when I'm not expecting him. Especially in the middle of the night.

He throws back our bed covers, "Checking for cheats."

We are in our nighties. He looks disappointed and marches out of the room. Earl hasn't tried cheating either by the sound of it. There would have been an uproar if he had, and I don't hear a thing from his room. I think it has made Richard even more angry that none of us has tried to cheat, and I can't tell if he's gone back downstairs or not. He could be back at the bottom or he could be standing right outside my bedroom door - bursting in again at any second. I want to inspect my window to see how hard it will be to escape if I have to in a hurry. I daren't get out of bed though. Not until the whistle blows. I'll only make matters worse if he catches me.

A few minutes pass, but it seems like ages. He bursts into the room again to check for cheats. He looks even more frustrated this time, as no one is cheating - we've all worked him out. He leaves the room slamming the door. I hear him slam Earl's door and there is silence. For someone that thinks they're so clever and tricky, he is very predictable.

My sister and I lie waiting and waiting. Half an hour must have passed. I hope Earl hasn't fallen asleep.

The whistle sounds again. We jump out of bed and rush to get our uniforms on. I'm quick and help pull my sister's jumper over her head as she's pulling her socks on. We run, I grab her blazer, she holds her arms up; luckily it is too big for her and slides down onto her. I push her through the door in front of me as I pull my own blazer on. We run and get to the bottom of the stairs before he blows the wretched whistle again. He is looking at a stop watch. I am looking up the stairs and willing Earl to hurry. Richard blows the final whistle and Earl appears at the top of the stairs in his uniform. He doesn't even attempt to come down. He just turns and goes back to his room.

Richard is livid. He starts screaming again in his stupid, high pitched, nasally sergeant's voice. My sister and I run up the stairs and back to our beds. I wonder how long Richard can keep this up. I guess we're going to continue this exercise until we get it right.

After the sixth time my sister starts to cry. We both realise that it is hopeless, as no matter how quickly we get to the bottom of the stairs, Earl hasn't got there on time once yet, and I don't think he is ever intending on getting there.

After seventeen attempts, my sister and I are told to go back to bed and stay there until we are told otherwise.

Now it's between Earl and Richard. By the sound of it Earl never gives in. I don't hear him leave his bedroom once until after the second whistle has been blown. Richard must be close to killing him. I think Earl is actually enjoying every moment that he torments Richard.

Richard is not going to be defeated though. As on all Sunday evenings, our uncle and aunty will be arriving soon, so we are told to get dressed and we'll continue the exercise another time - we will continue it until Earl shapes up and gets it right.

All this time my mum has been in the kitchen. She can hear what is going on I'm sure. I wonder why she doesn't take us away from here. Why she doesn't try harder to stop him being crazy?

The relatives turn up and Richard turns into a normal person, and we all pretend that we are all normal people in a happy family - a slightly better family than other families because we have more clocks. We have to smile otherwise we'll get in more trouble.

Memory of a Free Festival
Monday.

I get home from school on Monday afternoon. I'm pissed off that I can never enter the park again, but surprised that Richard isn't home. It is really odd and unnerving. Even the static charge that he creates has gone out of the house. He is unemployed and he is always here; he never goes out anywhere, like to the pub or, well, just anywhere. He hasn't got any friends to go to visit. My first instinct is that it is some kind of a trick. Maybe he is hiding somewhere; maybe in the house or outside waiting to jump out at me and chop me up and eat me, like in my worst nightmares.

Then another thought enters my head; a much more positive and exhilarating thought. Maybe he is seriously ill or injured in hospital. He might have been run over horribly, and is still just alive but paralysed from the neck downwards. The thought of that takes me back to the days of pulling wings off of ladybirds and legs off of spiders to see if they could still move as fast, not realising that they were a living feeling creature and it would really hurt them. Richard isn't a living, feeling creature though. I could have some fun. I could get the bastard back; I could make his life hell. I could get a poisonous pet snake and starve it nearly to death then throw it on to Richard. If he's paralysed, he won't be able to move. It'll bite him, and kill him, and swallow him whole. I could say it escaped by accident so I wouldn't get put in prison. There is a catch though; I won't be allowed a poisonous pet snake in the house. The thought excites and strengthens me all the same. Then I realise that it doesn't seem enough. Richard actually deserves worse than to die - worse than to be eaten alive.

After an hour of trying to figure out what is going on or what the trick is, I finally ask my mum where he is. This approach might be part of the trick, but the suspense is killing me.

Unfortunately for me, he is not in hospital after a nasty paralysing accident, but fortunately for me it isn't a trick (that I will receive a punishment for, due to the length of time that it took me to ask the question). He has had to go away on a government training course for unemployed people. It is called a TOPS course, and all unemployed people have to go on it or they get their dole money stopped. If we don't get any dole money, we won't have anywhere to live, and then we'll end up being homeless. I've heard it a thousand times before. I am told this by my mum who has been instructed and brainwashed by Richard. I can live with this outcome though. I might even get put into a children's home.

The reason I hadn't been told about this course prior to today, is because I might have planned to do something disruptive and upset my mum, and my brother, and my sister. The less I'd known about it the better, for everyone in Richard's eyes.

I'm still extremely happy about it; I have a week to prove that I am normal, and my mum will see that she can cope without Richard being here. She might even enjoy it. She will see that I'm not a problem child, or a liar. I have no intentions of upsetting my mum - quite the opposite. She might even realise that it is Richard that is the problem, but I think it would still have been better for everyone if he'd have got paralysed.

I think that my mum is glad that he isn't here in a way, but she already looks stressed; like the responsibility of holding it all in place is a little too much for her. It's him that has put all that shit in her head. The responsibility of trying to do Richard's job to keep him satisfied, and not make him angry, must be a difficult and stressful demand on her. I hope that, at least for this week, she won't be walking around on eggshells like she does all the time, or begging me not to upset Richard.

So my first question to the woman is, obviously, "Can I go out?" The answer should be a simple, 'yes' or 'no'.

Instead I get a recital. It goes something like this.

'You can go out, but I need to know where you are...
Just in case Richard rings up and asks me...
I won't cover up for you if you lie...

He'll know if you're lying, you know he'll find out...

So, oh, and don't be late, please, please don't be late...

Because he's bound to ring, please, please don't be late...

If he rings and you're not here, he'll get worried...

And when he gets worried he gets angry, and well...

You know what he's like when he gets angry...

Then he'll travel back and not be able to do the course...

If he doesn't complete the course, well, oh God...

Then the government will stop our money...

Then we'll end up homeless...

Think of your brother and sister...

I am nodding at her and getting closer and closer to the front door with each line. I know the bloke is doing a good job fucking around with my head - what he is doing to my mother's is sad, but she's a grown up, and she's big enough to change things. I can't wait to be a fucking grown up.

I take hold of my handlebars and walk my bike out of the front door. She is behind me still wittering about getting back on time and Richard. I want to turn around and shake her, and tell her to fucking shut up. I want to hit her and scream that he's not here, but I want to get out of this fucking house even more. I slam the door closed behind me and I'm off; I am free. I ride down the street as fast as I can, but only for a short way. My bike doesn't feel right. My bike is almost part of me, and I know something isn't right with it at all. I look down at the road and notice that the front wheel is really wobbling around. It's never been like that before and I know that I haven't damaged it in any way. I stop and I get off. I take hold of the front wheel and shake it. It's really loose. I lift the bike frame, only a couple of inches off of the road, and the front wheel falls clean out spiralling forward, around and landing in the gutter. I know exactly who's done this and why, but who will believe me? Nobody will believe me; same as nobody will believe that he tampered with my gears, that he'd tampered with my brakes, that he tampers with my mind and he tampers with my body. One day I will make people believe me; they will know that I have never been a liar.

My wheel needs fixing and fast. The closest place I can think of that might have a spanner I can borrow, without going back home, is the newsagent in the next street. So I defiantly stick the wheel back in place, and I push my bike down the alley, up the next street and into the shop.

Mr. Brown, the newsagent, is standing behind the counter in the shop expecting me to buy a pencil probably.

"*Why a pencil?*"

'I have to get my pick fixed. I haven't time for

your questions.'

"Tell me and I'll leave you alone."

'Okay. On Richard's birthdays my mum gives us all a few pence to go to the shop to buy Richard something nice. Richard only has one joke that he laughs at aloud to himself, and he always expects us kids to laugh too. No matter how many times we hear it, we know we must laugh. It is: What did the constipated mathematician do? The punch line is: He worked it out with a pencil. Not funny, so don't laugh! So every birthday I take my brother and sister to Mr. Browns shop, and with our pennies I always buy Richard a pencil. I get Earl and my sister to get him a jotter, a pencil sharpener or a rubber. Every year Richard asks me why I always buy him pencils. Every year I want to respond with, "Work it out." But every year, I'm too scared to.'

"I didn't laugh."

'Good. Now go away."

I don't really know Mr. Brown very well. His wife sometimes works behind the counter, and he's not about in the shop much himself. I hope he is today. It's a lovely shop; it's like most newsagents used to be with the newspapers all over the counter, jars of sweets strewn along bent shelves waiting to be weighed out, and bottles of pop lining the edges of the walls and the counter. He doesn't sell tea, coffee, and bread and all the other things that the other shops sell now. He just sells fags, and sweets, and pop, and newspapers, and pencils.

I walk in with my bike pleased to see Mr. Brown standing there. I apologise that I'm not here to buy anything, but that I can't ride my bike, as it is broken, and I need some help. He is really happy to help me. He goes out to the back of the shop to get the right sized spanner. While he's away, I grab three bottles of lemonade that are in front of the counter on the floor. I run outside and stuff them into a hedge then I run back into the shop. He appears again with a spanner. I go to take it from him. He smiles at me, shakes his head and says, "I'll do it. I'll make sure it's nice and tight. I wouldn't want you having an accident."

He notices that the nut on the back wheel is also dangerously loose - he tightens that too. "Looks like sabotage to me," he says, raising his eyebrows. I know it's bloody sabotage, but I smile naively. He has fixed my bike. I think I like him. I am so happy - even my bike looks happy.

Then he says, "How old are you?"

My smile turns to a frown. He is really old; I have a dilution dilemma. I really don't want any old pervert to fuck me just to dilute Richard. It is defeating the whole point of diluting old fucking, sad, evil, bastards.

The thought of Mr. Brown wanting to fuck me just makes me freeze. I am still looking at him with my frown and my eyes fixed. I sense myself slowly curling up into a little ball and retreating into the very small place in the back of my head.

He must have noticed my withdrawn look, or

maybe he didn't. He catches my attention back by waving his hand in front of my face, and he continues, "Because if you're over thirteen years old, you might consider doing a paper round. I have a morning and an evening round available. They are large rounds, but not that many papers. Having a bike would be an advantage. What do you say?"

I'm still recovering from my evasion, but I swallow a sigh of relief and return to the real world. It is really strange. He is an old man and he speaks to me like, I guess, a child should be spoken to. He speaks to my face not to my tits (that had appeared from nowhere overnight once, and I have been trying to hide them under big jumpers ever since). His eyes are kind, genuinely kind.

"I'll do both, but I have to check with my mum."

"I'll get you the route lists. You can take them home and show your mum." He laughs, nods and goes out to the back of the shop again to get the lists for the rounds. While he is away, I pick up four bottles of cherryade. I run outside and hide them in the bush with the lemonade then shoot back in. He comes back into the shop with the list of streets and houses in order of delivery. I know all of the streets, but I notice that they're in a weird order. I decide I'll change it later - I can change everything, later.

All I have to do now is convince my mum that it's a good thing, and she will have to tell Richard.

Mr. Brown nods his head, which he does all

the time, awaiting my approval. "Would you like someone to show you the route? I could drive you round it when Mel gets here."

I don't speak. I just hold up my thumb still studying the list. I walk towards the door - someone might steal my pop bottles. He calls out to me, "The shop will be shut in the morning. You'll have to come round to the back entrance about six thirty." I expected something like that - I shudder.

So I'm out, I'm free, I've got two jobs and I've already memorised the rounds. At this minute though, my only concern is pulling those bottles of pop out of the bush and turning them into glue. I sneak back to the bush and I take hold of three of the bottles. That's good they're still here and nobody has seen me. Holding my bike in the other hand, I walk the street for a bit before turning the corner to be out of view of the main road. I take off the bottle tops and pour the lemonade into a storm drain in the road. All three of them empty, I screw the refundable marked tops back on. I carry them back to the main road and push my bike to the Co-op with the empties under my arm. The lady gives me thirty pence for them at the counter.

Great, I have my thirty pence and four more bottles in the bush. I cycle back to Mr. Browns shop. I pull the cherryade bottles from the bush. I struggle a little - pushing my bike and clinging on to four bottles is a little trickier than three, and they're worth nothing smashed. I head up the main road again, turn the corner and stand over the drain. The cherryade flows down the drain slowly, too slowly. The more I try to shake it out, the slower it flows. The pink froth, that's being produced, is close to emerging over the drain cover, and I still have two bottles to go.

A scruffy boy appears from nowhere. He's about the same age as me, and he's walking towards me. He's pale, malnourished and spookily haunted looking. He stops right in front of me and asks, "What you doing?"

I'm not one for conversation, so I just reply, "Fuck off."

He doesn't move. He just stands staring at the drain, as I pour the next bottle away.

"Fuck off." I say again, but louder. This time he turns and walks away entering a rotten looking house across the road. I can't believe his cheek - he freaked me out a bit. I can see, from the corner of my eye, that he is still watching me from the window this time. I don't directly look his way. I continue with the last bottle, as the gully in the road fills with pink froth. He still watches; he really is very strange.

I can't take these bottles to the Co-op as well; they'll get suspicious of me. I can't take them to Mr. Brown's shop either; he'll realise that I stole them, as half a row of bottles has gone missing from in front of his counter. The glue shop is too far to walk, but I don't fancy trying to ride my bike carrying four glass bottles, and if I drop one I won't have enough money for a single tube of glue. I look down at the bottles, my bike, my hands, my fingers - there is a way. I take the lids off all the bottles, putting them in my pocket. I stick each finger on my left hand into a bottle squeezing my fingers together. I lift my hand and the bottles stay on; hanging there they seem pretty secure. I rest my hand on the handle bar and let the bottles dangle from my fingers. It looks dodgy, but what choice do I have. My right hand will have to do the braking. Once I feel comfortable that they aren't going to slip off, even over bumps in the road, I ride off to the glue shop - not as fast as I can, but very, very carefully.

It isn't really a glue shop, and it isn't even really a hardware shop. It's a sweet shop, newsagent, grocery store, video rental, tobacconist, off licence, post office, birthday card, gift shop and it always has a plentiful supply of glue, so long as the man behind the counter believes your reason for wanting it, and your parents haven't threatened to kill him. I take my bike into the shop with me, and I lean it against his counter, he rolls his eyes up and tuts, as usual.

I take out my thirty pence and place it on top of the newspapers on the counter. I pull the bottle tops from my pocket and place them on the counter with the money then raise my left hand high onto the big pile of newspapers, so that the bottles stand upright. I pull each finger out, steadying the bottles with my other hand. My middle finger has swollen, so it is too big to slide out as easily as it had slid in. I twist and pull at it for a minute or so, as the shop man takes the other bottles out of harm's way. Out pops my finger and I pass him my final ten pence bottle. It isn't too much of a drama. Though it did flash through my head that I might have to cut my finger off. I need that ten pence bottle more than I need a finger.

I ask for a tube of glue. The man knows exactly what I am going to ask for; I have never bought anything else from his shop. He asks me what I want it for. I reply, "I'm making an aeroplane." He gives me the tube and a penny change. As I'm leaving, he shouts at me, "Leave your bloody bike outside next time." I hold my thumb up and nod.

Right, I have the glue, but I don't have a bag. I ride to the park as fast as I can push the heavy gears. It's a fair way, and I don't have that much time. I ride as fast as the cars are driving. It feels good as I pass some rich freak on a new, streamline racing bike with skinny tyres. He's wearing a fancy helmet, tight black cycling shorts and funny shoes. I don't just pass him - I fly past him like the wind. He'll probably try to catch me up now, they try to do that sometimes, I must really piss them off. I hit a pothole in the road. Fuck, my rims! Then I remember - if I hadn't noticed the nut was undone earlier, and got it fixed when I did, more than my rims would have been fucked up. I'd be splattered all over the road right now; I have survived another Sabotage attempt.

I reach the park. The fancy cyclist hasn't been able to catch me up, and he won't be going my way anyway. I mount the kerb and ride down the steep hill towards the duck end of the lake. A bloody fly hits me straight in the eyeball, but even he isn't going to slow me down. I press my finger into my eye - holding it shut until I reach the lake. Tears are streaming down my face, but the dead fly has worked its way to the corner, and I scrape him out with what finger nail I have, and flick his nasty body away. Strangely, I can still smell him in my eye.

Although my vision is blurred, I can already see that the bins have been emptied. Unbelievable! No, believable - just my luck - there isn't a single bread bag in either bin. There aren't even any bags blowing around or floating in the lake. I check the surrounding bushes, but nothing. I ride on dismayed, but not defeated. I ride down to the spinney, even if there's no one there to help, there will be old dried up bags or discarded ones with holes in that I can knot.

I ride around the lake with only one thing on my mind - to the spinney. I pass the fisherman that I met before briefly. I take no notice this time, and don't even give him a 'hello'. I get to the spinney and push my bike through the bushes to where the dope-heads and glue-sniffers hang out. There is rubbish and glue bags strewn everywhere, in the bushes and squashed amongst the leaves on the ground. It's quite a disgusting sight from where I'm standing. After rummaging through all the mess for a while, I find a bag that is passable, useable, and still quite fresh. It hasn't been squashed solid and set. It isn't a Sunblest bag, but beggars can't be choosers.

There's a huge log in front of me - well, it's an uprooted, dead tree to be correct, it'll make a good seat. I climb up onto it and fill the bag with my tube of honey. It takes longer than a nice easy pot.

I kiss the bag. It's strange to think that, sometime earlier, someone else was here kissing the same bag. I probably knew them, so it's ok.

As the buzzing begins and the filthy landscape before me turns beautiful, I sit and wonder. I try to figure out how a tree so big, compared to all the others around it, ended up uprooted and lying here. There's a big sandy hole in the ground full of broken roots, like a moon crater, where the tree had once stood. Surely if the wind had knocked it down, it would have knocked all the other smaller trees, with smaller roots, down too. It doesn't look like it's been struck by lightning; it isn't burnt. Something brought it down, as big as it is. It's just lying here, ripped roots in the air, dead, barkless and leafless - only a hole where it once stood proudly, and I have climbed up to sit on it. I'm more powerful than a big tree.

The buzzing is so intense that I stop thinking about the big dead tree, and I float with it for a while until, from behind me, a leaf touches my shoulder. It taps at me like a Morse code machine. I turn around to see where it's coming from. It is reaching to me from a very lively bush that's thriving behind my seat. The bush hums and sways in the light breeze. It has long finger-like leaves - five at the end of each branch and twig. One branch is stretching out hard and tapping a message on my shoulder with a leaf finger. I only know SOS in Morse code, so I don't understand what it is trying to tell me.

"I don't understand." I say to the bush. The bush continues to hum. The hum turns into a rhythm, the rhythm to a chanting. A spooky, whispering tune fills the air around me. I try to ignore it, and keep breathing in my bag, but it keeps touching and tapping me, and the rhythm and the whispering are now a hundred tiny voices chanting in time with each other. A chant that is repeating itself, "Remember the hippies." Over and over, "Remember the hippies."

I'm getting pissed off with the poking. I'm annoyed with myself that I'd never learnt Morse code fully. I can't relax properly for fear of falling off this dead tree, and I don't even know any hippies, so how can I remember them. I'm confused and irritated by the whole situation.

I turn to face the bush and give it an aggravated stare. Its hand is reaching straight for my face now. Its finger touches and taps me between the eyes, and its chant booms, "Remember the hippies."

Fear takes over me. I jump down from the dead tree log. I pick up my bike from the glittering littered ground. I want to run, but I don't want to show my fear, so I make myself walk calmly away. I look back to make sure the arms of the hippy bush don't stretch out to get me.

I push myself through a twiggy bush, and the fisherman that I know vaguely is standing right in front of me. He smiles and speaks to me, but I can't hear him. I unusually drop my bike into a twiggy bush. I grab him and hug him - I look back again at the weird hippy bush. It's ok. It isn't chasing me.

He holds me and asks me stuff, but it doesn't make any sense to me. It doesn't matter; I know that he is concerned about me. He keeps a hold of me for a while, kisses the top of my head, strokes my hair, and makes me feel safe.

He fucks me. I think while I'm still standing up - I could be lying down, it's hard to tell. Everything is swirling around me and it's a bit of a blur. Sky, green, leaves, sky, rubbish, green, bike, the glue is wearing off. Sky, green, Bike, Bike, Bike! The fisherman picks my bike up out of the bush with me clinging to it, and he pushes us out of the spinney. He still looks concerned, and he's still trying to say something that I am not registering. I get on my bike. I have to get home and quick. Having to ride on the main road, I need to get myself together, and pretty sharpish. I'm not that bothered at the moment if I get killed on the road. I have diluted Richard a little more without even trying, or being aware of it.

I ride like I am invincible, and luckily come to

no harm. I just don't want to be late. I want to prove to my mum that I'm not all of the things that Richard makes me out to be. Even though he seems to be doing a good job of manipulating my mind, and I am actually turning into the person that he's been saying I was all along. How I see it is: if you're going to get blamed for something anyway, you might as well do it.

I am going to be late though, but only five minutes or so. It might as well have been five hours. I've disappointed myself, and Richard isn't even here.

Opening the front door, I come face to face with my mum in the hallway. She's hovering near the telephone. Her eyes are wide and wild, and full of fear and tears. She starts making desperate crying noises, and waving her arms about - shaking like a hippy bush. I can't understand her. Her voice mixes with the glue. It makes all the words from her mouth a load of gobbledy-gook. I just stand looking at her; it seems like ages. I can't and daren't try to speak. I just stare at her mouth trying to make out what the words are that must be coming out of it. I can still hear a voice chanting away in the distance, and telling me to remember the hippies. The little logic - that has crept back - tells me that this is not coming out of my mum's mouth. Now that would really freak me out.

She calms down eventually, and I am slowly getting back to normal. I think about how this man can have turned my mum into this quivering wreck.

What has he done to her? She was never like this when I was small. Whatever it is, it has just made me a little more determined that he isn't going to do it to me. I am getting older and braver, especially now, now that he isn't here.

At last, we can both finally speak properly. I tell her that I've got the jobs at the paper shop. I hold out the list of houses that I have to deliver to, hoping for a smile, a look of pride on her face, anything positive, I get anything but.

This only starts her off again.

She holds her head in her hands in despair and protests that I've done this on purpose this week because 'he' isn't here, and how it isn't fair on her to ask him if I can do the paper rounds and on and on and on she goes.

God, I want to slap her round the face properly. Yeah, I am scared of the bastard too. I have been for the last seven years but he isn't here and she's a fucking grown up; well she used to be.

My mum looks at me like she hates me; like I'm the evil one causing her all this hassle. I choose not to speak again. I walk past her and begin to climb the stairs. A little bit of me searches for a pattern in the plain carpet, and the phone rings.

I want to keep walking up the stairs, but I freeze. I don't want to speak to him.

I can hear though. I can hear her telling him that I have only been a few minutes late, and she asks him if he wants to speak to me - to prove to him that I really am here, and that she isn't covering up for me. I want to shout down so that he hears me, so that he knows she is telling the truth without me having to speak to him personally, but that will only upset my mum. Luckily he doesn't want to speak to me; he believes her confirming to her that he knows when she's telling the truth and when she's lying.

She puts the phone down with a big sigh, and wanders off into the kitchen shaking her head. I walk quietly back down the stairs and into the living room. I know the clock faces are all staring and frowning at me, so I keep my gaze away from them. The television is on, and my brother and sister are still up. It's a lot later than they're usually allowed up. I guess they're taking the piss and taking advantage that Richard isn't here.

My mum hasn't noticed because she's been too worried about me being late, or maybe she has just let them carry on because they are never any trouble.

I sit down in front of the fire at the foot of Richard's armchair and the shadow of his grandfather clock. I sneak a sly glimpse at the pink knots, and it doesn't seem so imposing.

This is the only warm place in the whole house at any time of year. I stare at the television, but I'm not watching or listening to it. I don't even realise that I am getting burnt. I am just sitting thinking about what our lives could be like if Richard didn't live with us. I look at Earl and my little sister glued to the television set, not speaking to me, not speaking to each other, just staring straight at it. I think they watch so much television to escape really being here, or maybe they're cold too and want be near the fire. It is warm - it is very warm. I don't watch television much because I don't want to sit at the foot of Richard's big armchair, with his moccasin slippers rubbing against me, with the waft of his repulsive farts intruding into my nose and with his big fucking granddaddy clock watching me waiting for my mum to go out, and to hear that rat infested voice say, 'Get upstairs NOW'.

There is a couch in the living room but it is pushed up into the bay window at the farthest point from the fire. It is draughty and you can't see the television properly from it because the angle of the television is pointing towards Richard's big armchair. Well fuck that. I'd rather go without telly.

I realise that I am sitting too close to the fire. My leg is seriously burning. The skin is red and blotching, but I look back at the television, as if the leg isn't mine, and the pain stops. The fire keeps on burning.

Open coal fires always look nice on Christmas adverts. Yet ours is an intense, spitting fire of very old, dead wooden and plastic feet that my grandfather had collected.

"Your grandfather collected old wooden feet? That sounds like an odd hobby."

'It's not like that. My grandfather worked in a shoe factory all of his life, as most old people around here did. When these things called 'lasts' were replaced, due to wear and tear, my granddad would take them home to recycle them. Then, when the factories closed down, as they all ended up doing, he took all the lasts rather than seeing them thrown into the skip. It's just a foot shaped lump of wood. Some are one solid piece, and some are two pieces with a bendy part in the middle. Some are all wooden, and some are wood and plastic. They're moulds to make shoes. Really rich people had their own feet cast in plaster, and a last made only for their shoes. Unless something drastic happened to their feet, they'd always get a perfect fitting pair of shoes. Anyway, my granddad has a house full of wooden feet. Our house has a small walk in cupboard full of wooden feet, and the fire, that keeps this small part of the house warm, is kept burning by, what look like, burning human feet.'

I glance back down at my leg and notice it is blistering. I wonder if it would burn like a wooden foot does if I put it in the fire. I look at all the feet stacked up waiting to be burnt, and I don't care that my leg stings each time I look at it. It has gone past the initial warning pain; the pain that makes your eyes stream and causes an unconscious action to pull away. I shut my eyes and go to the place, in the back of my mind, where I go when Richard wants me; I can't feel the burn now. I can't feel my body at all. It's almost as if I have left it. It's good practice for Richard's return. Common sense finally prevails, and I move away slightly. A trip to the hospital is not worth the trouble it'll cause.

I don't want to be in this room anymore. My leg will only hurt now if something touches it, it has gone completely numb. I throw five more lasts onto the fire before leaving the room. I see the nervous, frightened eyes of my brother and sister. They look at me for a split of a second then they look back to the television. At this moment, I don't give a fuck if the whole house burns down and we all get frazzled. I hate this stupid fucking hell house and everything in it.

"You don't really mean that do you? I thought you were stronger than that," The voice in my head asks.

He's right, and I remind myself that I do give a fuck if I die tonight. I have a reason to live; I have things to do in the future. And there is no way that I am going to die before Richard. Only moments ago, I was close to giving in. Now, within seconds, thanks to my mysterious friend, I want to be here to watch him die. If the house is going to burn down, it's going to be while he's in it. I want to be the last fucking voice that he ever hears - 'Welcome to hell.' I have to survive to become a grown up, to paint his fucking grandfather clock pink, to deface the sun dial at the bottom of our street, and there'll be more things - good things for me.

In Richard's absence I have strength again. I have goals and I have a future to look forward to, a bright, free future.

I go to my room, lie on my bed and stare at the ceiling. I scan it like a telescope searching the heavens, hunting for - 'The dragon, The giant snail, The major skeleton jaws of a shark, The minor skeleton jaws of a shark and The granny with a knot in her hair' - on the artexed ceiling, like a stargazer searching the sky for constellations. They are all still here; nothing changes.

"Is your granddad dead now?"

"No he's not, nor's my Nan, but I don't see much of them anymore. They always looked after me if my mum was busy, when I was small, before Richard came along. They stopped looking after me when my mum met Richard. He said they didn't need to anymore. Things started going missing when we visited them. Money and small, but obvious, things. I was blamed. I knew it was Richard, but who would believe me over him. He told them that I was a liar and a thief, and I couldn't be trusted. They must have realised that this miraculous change had only occurred when Richard arrived in our lives. They knew me for six years before all this. They used to teach me card games. I learnt to knit socks and gloves. My Nan had a serious stamp collection that she'd let me look at, and I'd ask questions about the places that they came from, so long as I didn't touch them with my fingers. When I stayed there over night I was able to crawl in between them in the morning in their bed. I could cuddle up to both of them. I preferred my Nan because my granddad, and his pillow, always smelt of the greasy stuff that he put on his hair. Everyone was sane and normal, or so I thought. My Nan was apparently mad. I can't say I believe whoever diagnosed her as mad - it was probably Richard. I admit she did used to speak to her next door neighbour, Pauline, quite frequently even though she had been dead for some years. Many times I've been with her when she talked to Pauline, and there was definitely a two way conversation going on. After Richard came on the scene, I never stayed with them again. He's convinced everyone that I'm trouble, a liar and a load of other bad stuff that I don't even know about. My granddad believes him. I can tell by the disappointed look he gives me whenever he sees me. I don't think my Nan takes him seriously, but she lets life carry on, and has never got involved. My mum told me once that my Nan wasn't quite right because, when she was young, she had electricity shot through her brain. She says Nan is schizophrenic and hears voices. I find it hard to believe that one of the nicest, wisest, wittiest people that I know is regarded like this by someone who chooses to live with a proper fucking weirdo, pervert, schizo herself. Maybe it's my mum who's mad, and it's another excuse for Richard to use against us - it's genetic and we're all the mad ones not him.'

I try to stop thinking about it which isn't hard, as I can hear my mum crashing around in the kitchen below me. She spends so much time in there - finding things to do. Probably because she doesn't want to sit at the bastard's feet and watch television either.

Sitting on my bed, the feeling is coming back to my leg. It is pulsating like a cartoon thumb that's been struck by a huge hammer. To distract myself from it, I pick up a pen and two pieces of paper. At the top of one I write TOPS, and the other I write YTS.

It is a strange time. If you're not at school, you are on a training scheme of some kind. No one actually goes to work anymore.

I've been told that the courses are Maggie's way of making the unemployment figures look smaller. I am told that nobody actually learns anything that will help them get a job because there aren't any jobs to get.

I'm just happy that Richard has had to go away for a week on a course. It's like a holiday for me; my first break in seven years.

I look at the pieces of paper and I wonder what TOPS and YTS stand for, and I begin to write out two lists.

Y.T.S. This is the course that Pat, my skinhead friend and diluter is on.

        Young Troubled Skinhead
        Yellow Tube Sniffer
        Yobs Thieving Scheme
        Your Tattooed Skin
        You Terrible Scum

Young Toothless Slaphead
You're The Scrag
You Two Schizos
Young Tight Strides
Yell till sunrise
Yell till sun-up
Yet to sting

T.O.P.S. This is the course that Richard is on.

Twatty Old People's Scheme
Touchy Old Perverted Sicko
Tinkering Old Paedophiles Stink
Thatcher's Operation for Penis Shrivelling
Thatcher's Official Paedophile Slayers
Toothless Octopus Pant Stain
Tastes Of Paint Stripper
Try Our Pet Snake
Tastes Of Pungent Sprouts

Both lists are getting long and pretty bizarre, but it passes some time away. I hide them away in a box marked private along with my dilution formulas. They are looking very much to my advantage. I understand them although they look like something that Einstein would scrawl all over a blackboard in a university. They make perfect logical sense to me. They are my only solution to my problem. I can't do anything to stop this shit, not until I'm grown up, or until I find somebody, in this world, that will believe me and rescue me and protect me. I don't believe in miracles though. All I can do is to keep the damage as diluted as possible.

My sister comes in and gets into bed. I don't speak to her that much anymore. She's my closest relative, in the same room as me, and we don't speak. We used to when we were really young. We'd play together, I'd read her stories and show her how to make things, but now, no one talks to each other. Everyone walks on eggshells - be careful what you say, be careful what you touch, where you look and who you look at, how many times you've flushed the toilet. Everything I do, I am pulled up and checked on it. If I answer a reason to something that I did or why I did it - I am told that I'm lying and I'm told the real reason why I did it. Richard tries to make me believe him. He wants me to believe that I don't know what or why I do things, and that only he knows everything about me. I've worked this one out and I'm not falling for it. Others may believe him. I'm not mad enough to have lost my sense of self, not quite.

As I'm am about to play my David Bowie album again, I hear music coming from a neighbouring garden. It reminds me that I've a job to do. I creep downstairs and get a screwdriver from the cellar. My mum is making a racket on a sewing machine in the kitchen. I go back to my room and undo the screws that seal my window. I open the rotten, rickety sash window with a struggle, and nosily look around for the source of the music. Some lads, who live a couple of doors down, are having a party in their garden. It's not their garden, of course, it's their parents' house. They have alcohol and the music is really loud, so I guess the parents have gone away. I watch through the window. They're happy, they're drinking, they're talking, they're laughing and they're in their parents' garden, bizarre. It is like watching something from a different world. I wouldn't be allowed to have friends round, even if I had some, they wouldn't be allowed to even wait for me in the hallway, never mind come to a party in the garden.

Then I see the lads' dad come out of their back door. I freeze waiting for the fireworks. I'm expecting all hell to break loose. He's wearing oven gloves and carrying a steaming tray into the garden towards a table. It looks like chicken legs and sausages from here. He's putting it on the table and sitting down with some of the lads, and opening a can of beer. I don't understand. This can't be real. It can't be normal. I really am totally bewildered as to why this man is acting like he's his son's mate and his mates' mate.

I watch in awe.

I watch, but I don't understand, until I'm not really looking anymore. My mind has wandered to imaging our garden full of people, and Richard making us sausages; it just wouldn't happen. Then again it might if he was planning to drag us one at a time into the garage and stuff the sausages up us the wrong way, just to please his sick cock. Hopefully it will never happen.

A voice finally catches my attention and breaks the spell.

I look down to where the voice came from. A lad is standing looking up at me and waving; he is in our garden. I panic and I try to pull the window shut, but it sticks. I have to push it back up to straighten it and try again. I tell him to fuck off in an angry whisper. He doesn't. The window is pissing me off. I get it down an inch, and it gets stuck. I push it up three inches, and he is still watching me. I tell him again quietly, but with a serious grimacing frown on my face, to fuck off out of our garden. Then I plead to him and I realise I sound like my mother - Afraid! Afraid of something, someone that isn't even here. I stop struggling with the window; I realise I must look crazy.

"Come and join us," he calls up.

I shake my head. I wouldn't be allowed to go anyway, and if I sneak out, without telling my mum, I'll be caught; it is too close to home. I keep shaking my head and step back away from the window, so that he can't see me anymore.

I sit on my bed and take the *'Scary Monsters'* album out of its sleeve. I shuffle toward the record player, along my bed on my bottom, so that I won't be noticed from the garden. I place the record onto the turn table and switch it on. Nothing happens; it isn't plugged in. I crawl under the desk to plug it in. A voice close behind me whispers, "Hey." I jump with fright, and hit my head on the desk. A face is peering in the window.

The lad from the party has climbed up the back of the house, and is smiling at me while hanging onto the outside of my window. I rush to him, grab him and help him through, only so that no one sees him hanging there. I would be murdered, for sure, if anyone tells Richard that they'd seen a lad climbing into my bedroom. Once he's in, I relax and giggle nervously; it's quite a funny situation. He looks shocked when he notices my little sister asleep in the bed next to mine, so I lift my quilt up over both of our heads. He fucks me in my bed. My sister is fast asleep and doesn't wake or stir, and my mum is downstairs fretting about the week ahead and thinking that I'm in bed, safe, reading. I'm not though; I'm diluting that fucking cunt of a husband of hers a little more, and feeling a whole lot better each time.

I hear my mum's footsteps coming up the stairs. Strange that, you never hear Richard coming. I throw the poor lad onto the floor with my legs. I whisper "Hide." He tries to roll under the bed.

My mum walks in. "What are you doing up here?"

"A big moth flew in and I threw a book at it."

"Well I'm surprised the room isn't full of

moths with the window wide open and the lights on." She heads towards the window.

I get up with the quilt around me and I step over the lad. "It's ok, I'll close it."

She tuts, turns and leaves the room. My little sister sleeps through it all.

I look down at the lad on the floor. He's frozen solid, and his eyes are tight shut like he is expecting a freight train to hit him at any second.

I whisper to him, "Come back to bed." I reach down to touch his head. He jumps which makes me jump. Realising the coast is clear, he's up, dressed, out of the window and down the drainpipe, as quickly as he was dragged through. He jumps over the garden walls, and re-joins the party. He doesn't even look up to wave goodbye. I close the window; it closes easily this time, without the panic. I replace the screws in case Richard comes home early and catches me.

I look down at their fucking great party. The music is rubbish and the lads are all ugly, spotty teenage idiots. There are a few girls that are probably related to them that no one would dare call, criticise or touch.

Everyone is friendly, smiley and perfectly relaxed. I could have climbed out of the window tonight and joined the party, after all, I had been invited. I have the freedom to have done it. I'm not scared of my mum, but I know that she gets terribly worried and really upset. There would have been shit when Richard got back if he'd have found out, but there will be shit anyway, whatever I do or don't do, it is inevitable. I wouldn't have wanted to join their party anyhow because I wouldn't have had a clue what to say or how to talk to any of those people. I have nothing in my head to share with them; nothing they would understand or be slightly interested in. The moans and gripes, which people generally take so seriously in their lives, seem insulting to me. Oh, what I could moan about? Nobody wants to hear real problems and nobody would believe me anyhow.

I can hear them now; they're talking about me. 'That's the weird girl who's always in a rush; who has no friends. She tells lies and makes up terrible stories for attention. Her poor family.

Luckily I need an early night.

Rebel, Rebel
Tuesday.

I get up early, and I'm really looking forward to doing my paper round. I know my bike will be safe to ride as Richard hasn't been here to tamper with it. I walk out of the front door; it's strange that I haven't had to get permission to leave the house. No one is behind me ready to stop or hinder me, and everyone else is asleep. If I wanted to, I could ride away for miles before anyone notices me missing. It's a thrilling idea, but I fear the trouble this would cause the rest of the family. Richard would come back early, he'd lose his dole money and they'd all end up homeless because of me. Richard would inevitably find me and punish me even more than usual, or maybe he'd just kill me. I close the front door behind me and ride off in the direction of Mr. Brown's shop.

It's still dark when I get to the paper shop - it's unrecognisable in the glow of a street lamp. I go around to the back of the shop, the way Mr. Brown had indicated, I can't even see the door that I'm meant to go to. I can see a slither of light peeping through a gap, it's a window. I tap on it. A door to the left of me opens and the light shines out. Mr. Brown's silhouette sends shudders through my body. He greets me, "Good morning," and walks back in. I follow him nervously without answering.

All the papers are sorted and packed into dirty, bright orange, waterproof bags, in the order on the list that he had given me. It feels strange being alone in a room with a man. He hasn't tried to frighten me or touch me. There is tension though; a tension that at any minute he might pounce. Mr. Brown doesn't seem to notice the charged atmosphere.

A boy walks in through the same door. Mr. Brown greets him too, but is only answered with a grunt. The boy picks up his paper bag from the floor beside a fridge and just walks straight back outside.

Mr. Brown shrugs. "That's Tim. Quiet boy."

I know exactly who he is. He's the boy that watched me tipping the cherryade down the drain across the road from his house. I hope he doesn't recognise me and say anything to Mr. Brown.

Well, I have my bag full of papers, I have my list, I leave the tension and ride off to do the round in the long-winded order that it is arranged in. It doesn't take too long on my bike. I agree that it wouldn't be a round that you'd want to walk. I return home for breakfast before leaving early for school. I don't want to be in this house any longer than necessary.

That is the whole point of having the paper rounds. It's not for the money - it's for the time away from that house. I settle by my bike in the bike sheds and wait for Jane to arrive with hers. She's bang on time, but says nothing to me. I leave her to lock my bike to hers and I go to my class.

At lunchtime I write out a new order for the

delivery round. One that will suit me better and to save me time. It doesn't matter if I change the order for the evening round because all the papers are the same and I can do them in any order I chose. Mr. Brown will have to sort the morning papers differently. I can't memorise who has what this quickly, but give me a few days and I will. I can't see it being a problem.

The school day is a drag. I should have freedom with Richard being away, but I fear he is somehow watching me.

After school I go straight to the shop for my evening round. I give Mr. Brown the list I've written up. "Would you mind sorting the papers in this order for the morning round? I think it makes more sense." I wonder if he thinks I'm being cheeky. Maybe I am; he might sack me. I find it difficult to know when I've said something right or wrong these days.

"Sure, so long as they get their papers and pay me, I don't mind what order you do it in." He takes the list from me before passing me the evening paper sack. It's all good; he doesn't think I'm rude.

Tim turns up just as I'm leaving the shop. He looks so miserable, his eyes acknowledge me, but I turn my head away, straddle my bike and ignore him. I know he must recognise, and now I'm really worried that he'll tell Mr. Brown that he saw me tipping the cherryade down a drain. Mr. Brown will know that it was me that had stolen his bottles of pop. He'll sack me for sure, and he'll tell everyone that I'm a thief. That'll please Richard, and he'll tell everyone that I'm a liar, and a thief, and a glue-sniffer. Everything is always against me. Nothing ever goes right.

The evening paper round is easy, but the anxiety of going back to the shop and getting called a thief exhausts my brain. Richard isn't even here, yet I feel the same about going back to the shop, as I do going home to that house. I need something to free me - I want to get out of it - out of my head. Glue! That'll do it. I need some strength and I must dilute Richard some more. I am so high when I've diluted him.

When I get back to the shop, nothing is said about the bottles. All my angst was pointless, but Tim may mention it tomorrow or next week. I'll have to get used to feeling like this every day.

I ride in to my street avoiding eye contact with the sun dial. I want to be happy to be back at home for a change because I know Richard isn't here. I say that confidently because that's how I really want to feel as I approach the door. I try to look like I mean it, but I actually have a gutting sense of dread, as I open the door and enter the house. The atmosphere is charged. I'm certain Richard is here. He's come back early - I'm positive. I bet someone had seen that boy leaving through my window. Someone might have rang the police thinking that he was a burglar and they'd been round and told my mum. Then she would have rang Richard and he would be back to punish me.

The dread envelops me. I crouch expecting something bad to hit me. I want so much not to feel like this all the time. It is me though. It's how it is, all the time, and it's probably how it'll always be.

I rest my bike against the hall wall under the clocking-in and clocking- out clock and close the door. I wait. No one is hovering in the hallway or doorways. There are no eyes watching and waiting. No nasally voice commands me where to go to, or fires questions at me.

I walk a prickly line along the hall and under the clock without a body into the kitchen. My brother and sister are sat at the dining table eating jam sandwiches, and my mum is washing up and throws something, that she had burnt earlier, into the bin.

Before I can speak, she turns around with that nervous face on. Earl and my little sister pick up on the tension. They go rigid and stare straight ahead of themselves. I know they're trying to cut off their hearing and I know it's all my fault. The whole room feels prickly and the ticking of the clocks slows, as I wait for her to speak. I imagine what she's about to say. She's spoken to Richard and I bet he's said, 'No she isn't going to do a paper round, and No she's still banned from the park, and No she's not going out at all, and No she should be stopped from breathing.'

To my utter amazement, that's not how it goes. Once the woman has composed herself, she speaks at last, "I spoke to Richard about the paper rounds. He's fine about it. He says it'll be good for you to realise the value of money. He is concerned that your school work will suffer because you'll be tired, so you'll only be allowed to go out twice a week. Mondays and Thursdays, and only till nine o'clock." She rushed the last sentence, as if she was scared of the response. I think it's strange. Is she becoming scared of everyone? Is my mum scared of me? Has Richard painted me so black that the woman sees me as something evil?

So there is a catch. I am only allowed out on Mondays and Thursdays, but I'll accept that. There's no point arguing. It's Richard's rule and she won't say any different. I nod at her, and she looks quite relieved that it's been that simple. The kids relax and continue to eat their sandwiches.

Once she is relaxed and contented that there'll be no conflict, I make myself a sandwich and without looking at her I say, "I don't really like going out on Mondays. I'm always tired on the first day of school, and doing the paper rounds is going to make it worse. I would have thought it would have made more sense to stay in on Monday. I always have the most homework on Mondays as well. Maybe he's forgotten about that. I think you should tell him Tuesdays and Thursdays would be better. You know, if he's concerned about school work." I sit at the table and eat my sandwich while she ponders my suggestion.

"It does make more sense," she finally

mutters. "I'll explain it to him later and I'm sure he'll be fine with it. It's only that he worries about you."

"I know. Tell him it was your idea. He won't worry so much then," I say, leaving the table. As I throw the crusts into the bin, I look at the burnt meal that she discarded earlier, but I can't figure out what it would have been. Whatever it was deserved being cremated.

As it is Tuesday, and I am only allowed out Tuesday and Thursday now, I'm going to make the most of it. I snatch my bike and call out, "Bye."

My mum starts wittering about time and Richard, pleading with me not to be late, but I'm out of the door. It is nice to be able to wave, and not to race away for fear of getting called back. Richard so often calls me back when my back tyre is still in the doorway.

'I will not be late,' I tell myself.

I ride to the Children's Home and call for Doris. I don't really want to see Doris; I have to dilute Richard some more while I have the chance. I could have gone straight round to Tex's flat, but he won't be home from work yet and I'd have ended up wasting the whole evening doing the washing up and vacuuming. That will only happen if I'm really desperate for somewhere to go and get out of the rain.

I knock on the door of the home and a very young social worker, Claire, answers the door. I walk in, and straight past her without saying a thing. She is very pretty and pretty useless. If these kids were real troublesome kids, she wouldn't stand a chance in this home. Luckily they aren't.

I'm glad Claire is working tonight; she sits in the office on the phone, all through her shift. She leaves the kids to do their own thing. I can go anywhere in the home when Claire is working; she doesn't care. Some of the social workers will only let visitors go into the television room and they check on you every five minutes - not today though.

I walk into the television room. Doris is lying horizontally in a chair, sideways. She looks in a bad mood which isn't unusual. She hardly notices me, and carries on watching the television. A young kid is sitting next to her. I don't know him; he must be new. They are watching *'Monkey Magic'*. Pat is doing all the actions to the program, and pretending he is Monkey trying to jump up onto clouds from his chair. Dan is watching Pat and laughing hysterically at him. This isn't quite what I had in mind for this evening, but it's making me laugh, and for once it's like being a real kid. Well it is until *'Monkey Magic'* finishes and I go down the corridor to the toilet. When I open the door to come out Dan is standing blocking my exit. He grins at me with his fat, rosy red cheeks looking rosier than usual. He pushes his way in. He quickly closes the door behind us. He fucks me against the toilet wall while I protest that I don't want to get caught and barred from the home. I definitely will if they find out what we're up to.

He assures me that it is only Claire on duty, and she won't leave the office all evening. He has finished by the end of the sentence and Richard has been diluted a little more. Everyone is happy.

I'm certain, that with Richard not being around, I can surely dilute him to nothing.

I decide to leave. Doris is in a really bad mood, and she hasn't spoken to me at all. Dan has fucked me and I am free. I tell them all that I have to go. This isn't unusual, they are used to me; I always have to go home early or am not allowed out at all. Pat waves to me and Dan gives me a cheeky wink. Doris carries on staring at the television.

I think I'll try Tex's flat now - he should be home from work soon. I ride as fast as usual though there really isn't any need. I have plenty of time. It's a habit.

Letting myself in, believing he's home, I lean my bike against the hallway wall. I can hear the television is on. It's a bit early for him to be home, but I'm so pleased he is. I run up the stairs to the living room to greet him, but he isn't here. His flat mate, Al, is sitting on the couch, and a very surprised looking girl is sitting in a chair. Her expression changes from surprised, to puzzled, to cross, as I freeze and stare at her.

I'm lost for words. Al stands up and puts his arm around me. "Hey Marie, this is Rachel - Tex's girlfriend. Rachel this is a very good friend of mine,

Marie." He pulls me down to sit on the couch with him, his arm still around me. "Rachel's been hearing stuff about Tex. She thinks he's got another woman. I've told her there's nothing to worry about." He laughs.

I'm burning up and scared to open my mouth. I force myself to smile and say, "He should be so lucky." Rachel's eyes roll and I realise I have probably just insulted her unintentionally.

Al looks uncomfortable about my remark. "I've told her she's got nothing to worry about, but she wants a serious chat with him. Don't you Rachel?" he calls over.

"Nice to meet you, Marie. I'd like some privacy when Tex gets in though."

"Sure." I rise with the intention of making a sharp exit. Al gets up too, and still with his arm around me, leads me out of the room. Calling back, "We'll leave you to it then. He shouldn't be long."

He takes me through to his bedroom and lets out a huge sigh. The door closes behind us and we sit down on his bed. We both start giggling, desperately trying to be quiet which makes it worse.

"Sorry, but I had to get you out of there. Imagine if Tex walked in and found you both sitting in the living room. He'd think he'd been caught out, and probably would have put his foot in it," he whispered.

"But my bike's in the hallway. He's gonna expect me to be here and then find her sitting in the living room. I should go. He might shout something before he spots her, and I don't want to be here if it gets nasty. I didn't really believe he had a girlfriend. I thought he just said that, so that I didn't expect any commitment from him. I don't want my hair being ripped out by her."

"Don't panic. Her car's outside. He'll see that before he sees your bike. It'll shit him up alright, but he could do with being taught a lesson. There won't be any trouble. I promise," Al says, as he begins to giggle again and pull me back on his bed. I lie back with him. He fucks me. It wasn't planned and I'd never thought of letting Al fuck me. It was perfect though - another dilution. Although I have no loyalty to Tex, I do feel a bit guilty when Al has finished. I get dressed quickly; I have no reason to hang around here any longer. The job is done - another dilution complete. There is no point in waiting for Tex.

"I have to go," I say, heading for the door.

"Aw, you're not gonna stay and listen to the fireworks?" Al asks.

I walk out of the bedroom and close the door behind me, without even answering. I pass the living room door swiftly and run down the stairs. I call out, "Bye," on my way out of the front door, and leave the guilt of both of them behind me in the flat. At least I didn't have to do the washing up this time.

The time is getting on, but it isn't time to go home yet. I don't really have the time to go anywhere else, so, for the first time ever, I go home a little early. I know Richard isn't here and it will please my mum, and stop her fretting at five minutes to nine. If she tells Richard though, it'll probably make him think that I've done it on purpose - to make it look like it is something to do with him. Well good, because it is something to do with him.

Getting in early, I'm expecting a pleased mother.

Instead a distraught woman is trying to shout at me, but it isn't loud. It's more like an angry whimpering. "You tricked me. You did it on purpose. I've spoken to Richard and he said I'm stupid. In fact he called me a lot worse things than that which are unrepeatable. Why do you have to make him angry? It's always you."

"What have I done?" I didn't really care to know.

"You tricked me. He said you could go out twice a week. Monday and Thursday. You tricked me to let you go out on today when you'd already been out on Monday. So, you think you'll be going out on Thursday as well? That's three days. Well you won't. Richard says you've been out twice this week already, so that's it. You're not allowed out until he gets home. You've tried to trick him too, and he's not happy about it. I knew this week was a mistake." She turns her back on me and heads towards the kitchen. I think she's crying.

So, now I've been out twice this week already

and I'm not allowed out anymore. It was worth a try. I'm not going to argue - what is the point? She'll only tell Richard. Is he trying to fuck my head up? Or is he trying to destroy my mum? Both is my honest answer. He has made me and my mum like aliens to each other.

I need a plan if I'm not allowed out until Richard gets back from his 'Time Out for Paedophiles Scheme'. I go up to my room to think of a way of getting out again this week. Nothing comes to me, so I pick up a book and read - it's called '*The Changeling*'. It's a little kids' story really - I used to read it to my sister when I used to speak to her, and when she used to listen to me.

It is only a short book but I like it. There's something about the story that makes me aware that my life is wrong. I like the bold pictures too - I loved painting when I was small.

I put the book back on the shelf and play my new LP. I lie on my bed listening and waiting for a plan to hatch. It is nice to know that I can go to sleep tonight when I want to, and that I can sleep with both eyes shut. Shut because I will really sleep knowing that I won't be disturbed.

A plan is forming of how I can continue my five days of relative freedom. It is quite simple really with a bit of persuasion.

China Girl
Wednesday.

I wake Earl up at six in the morning.

"Hey Earl. Do you want to earn some money?"

"What now?" He rubs his eyes.

"No not now. After school."

"Yeah, after school." He turns over and shuts his eyes.

"Meet me at Mr. Brown's shop straight after school."

Earl nods and goes back to sleep.

I know he's only ten years old, but he knows his way around the streets, and he could do with the money. I'm doing him a favour.

I do my normal morning round, and my usual mundane day at school. I overhear some interesting talk in the lunch queue. Apparently this Chinese girl is trying to beat the world record for the most fucks in twenty-four hours. A local nightclub is hosting the event at the weekend and they're looking for men to volunteer to help her. One girl said that her brother was already on the list. I don't know if they're telling the truth. It sounds outrageous that it would be allowed, but I haven't been able to get it out of my head all day. My mind's still trying to imagine the scene when I arrive at the paper shop. Earl is waiting for me. What a good boy!

I collect my newspaper bag full of the local

evening paper; it's very light, not much could have happened. I take the bag and Earl around to the side of the shop. I hand him the list. "This is half the round. Do you know where you're going?"

"Yeah, course I do. I'm not stupid," he replies and takes the bag.

"I know you're not. If anyone asks how old you are, just tell them you're thirteen."

"I'll tell them I'm helping my sister. No one's gonna believe I'm thirteen. Where's your bag?"

"I'm going back in to get it. Go on, get going. I'm doing you a favour." I push him and he wanders up the road.

I have a strange sense that I'm being watched. I still can't figure out why I am being allowed to do these two paper rounds. If I'm not allowed out for the rest of the week, why I am allowed to get up at half-five or six o'clock in the morning and go out in the dark and do a paper round? It makes no sense. Then again my whole life has never made any sense.

I ride up the street to Tex's flat and let myself in. No one's home, but it is early yet. The kitchen is in the worst mess I have ever seen. I hadn't cleaned it yesterday, but how could it have got this bad? He'd obviously wined and dined his girlfriend and maybe half of the town. They must have used a different glass for every drink. Maybe they had a party; they're getting very lazy. Do they think fairies come while they're at work? It looks like they've been trying to create a world record for balancing the biggest pile of washing up without it coming crashing down.

I take out what is in the sink. I start filling it with hot soapy water. There is something really satisfying about cleaning and washing up. I love pulling the plug out afterwards, and watching all the filth and shit get sucked away down the plughole. One minute it's there, then it disappears forever and everything's clean and new looking.

As I'm drying the shiny, clean dishes and glasses, and putting them away into the correct cupboards, Tex walks in. He has a big smile on his face; he's always pleased to see me. I still feel like a burden to him though. What with letting myself into his flat, and wanting his attention the minute he gets home from work even though he's always happy to give it.

I look down at my watch. Although the time is set wrong, I know how wrong it is. I know I only have fifteen minutes before I have to be back at the shop. It might seem pointless having a watch purposely set wrong when I know how wrong it is, but it's the principle. It's my protest against time, clocks and Richard.

Time is never on my side, so I grab Tex's arm and I pull him towards the stairs. He's laughing, not at me, just in a nice way. We fall onto the bed, and he starts fucking me while I keep checking my watch. "Did you have a party last night?"

"Yeah. Sorry I didn't invite you. I couldn't really. It was an engagement party, spur of the moment thing, you know. I had to do it to clear up a few things. Al said he covered my back yesterday by saying you were his girlfriend. Thanks for going along with it. I could have got right in the shit."

I smile. I guess Al kept it quiet that he'd fucked me.

Tex finishes, grunts and says, "It's funny really. Al looked really embarrassed when Rachel said, in front of everyone, that his girlfriend looked like jail bait to her."

I haven't got time for small talk. Pulling on my clothes I say, "Well I'm glad you sorted your problems out. I've gotta go."

He utters an unconvincing chuckle, shaking his head.

I kiss him on the cheek, run down the stairs, two at a time, grab my bike and I'm off at a hell of a speed to the last street at the end of the paper round. I can see Earl at the bottom of the street. Great, he hasn't finished yet; so I ride down and help him finish the last few papers.

We pass the Children's Home on the way back to the shop. "If you ever finish your round before me, leave the bag in that purple bush in front of the home. Don't take it back to the shop cos' we'll both lose our jobs." I don't need to tell him to keep his mouth shut about doing the round, as he's smarter than he lets on. He doesn't even answer me. He hands me the bag and runs off.

I drop my bag back into the shop. I head home to update my dilution tables. I am doing really well. If I can keep this up then surely soon it will be like Richard has never fucked me at all. I play *'Scary Monsters'* over and over again; it seems to make the time pass by quicker and stops me thinking and feeling sad. I'm going to tape every David Bowie song that I hear played on the radio, and eventually buy every album that he has ever made. My thoughts quickly return to the Chinese girl who's going to get fucked by possibly hundreds of men in one day. If I did that there would be no way Richard could ever catch up. I'd have taken away all of his power. It would take him years to be of any significance again, and I'd be grown up by then and long gone. I'm jealous of the Chinese girl, and at the same time I wonder why she has decided to do this record-breaking attempt. Does she feel like I do? Is she desperately trying to dilute someone? The thoughts swirl through my head as I drift off to sleep.

Ashes to Ashes
Thursday.

I get up early with ease. I've been sleeping so much better this week. It's dark, but I'm getting used to the gates and the steps, so I get my round done fast. Back at the shop Mr. Brown is grinning in an awkward way. His head is bobbing more than usual. I tense up in expectation of something unknown.

"I've got a little favour to ask you. I say favour, but you'll get paid for it." He's squirming.

Oh God, no. I blankly stare at him.

"I was wondering if you'd mind doing Tim's round. He hasn't turned in this morning. I've tried ringing the house, but there's no answer. I'd do it myself, but I have to open the shop."

I let out the breath I was holding in. "Yeah, sure." I pick up the remaining bag, check the address on the first paper and exit sharply. I've got plenty of time to do the round if I go straight to school after. I don't want to go home first anyway. I can't get into trouble for it; I'm allowed to do paper rounds, so what's the harm?

About halfway through the round, as I run down the garden of a house where a large sounding dog is barking from the other side of the letter box, I see my mum standing at the gate. I close it quickly behind me, and look her in the eye. "What's up?"

"I was worried about you. I thought you'd be home by now. I rang the shop and he said I'd find you around here somewhere. Why's it taking you so long today? What if Richard had called?"

She never takes this much interest in my whereabouts when Richard is home. I'm a bit stunned by her appearance, but at the same time it could be very useful. "Well the first couple of days I had help. I was being shown the round. I'm on my own now, so it's gonna take twice as long. I can't do it any faster. I'm running as it is. I won't be late for school; I'll go straight there. I've gotta dash." She stands there with a look of despair and disappointment on her face as I ride away. I have lost the guiltiness of lying to her. She is also the enemy for making me live with Richard.

She'll tell Richard that she intercepted me on the round, and I was exactly where Mr. Brown said I would be. It's worked out perfectly. I'm not intending on doing Tim's round again but I've got more spare time for myself. What I can do with it, at seven o'clock in the morning, hasn't come to me yet, but I'll think of something useful. Tim has done me a favour; I'll have to make it up to him somehow.

The round finished I go straight to school. I'm not late, I don't learn anything, it passes slowly, and I head back to the shop to meet Earl.

What a shock I get, as I lean my bike against the shop front. There is a sign stuck in the window saying 'Morning and Evening paper boy or girl required'. So much for saying I was going to make it up to Tim. I bet he's told Mr. Brown about the bottles. I bet I've been sacked.

I walk in expecting to be blasted. Mr. Brown nods his head, but says nothing. Am I meant to collect my bag? I'm not sure what I should do, but silence isn't solving anything, so I ask him, "Why's there a sign in the window?"

"Well you're sure to hear soon enough from someone, or read it in the papers," he begins. Good it's nothing to do with me. I wouldn't get put in the paper for stealing a few bottles of pop. It's something serious judging by his face.

"Last night, Tim's father… you know Tim don't you?"

I nod, get on with it.

"Last night, his father murdered his mother. From what I've heard, he was arrested in the early hours this morning and the house is cordoned off. I guess Tim's gone to stay with relatives. I haven't heard from him, but I guess the last thing on his mind is his round."

A pang of some kind of feeling runs through me. I had only spoken to the kid once, and that was to tell him to fuck off, twice. I wonder where you go to when something like that happens. I wonder where I would end up if Richard was to kill my mum. I don't think I'd really care where I was sent, as long as Richard went to prison, and I never had to see him again, I'd be so happy.

He'd probably kill me as well though. If he

was going to get done for killing one of us, he might as well kill all of us. It isn't as impossible an idea as it sounds - it could happen this weekend. Realistically, it is me that he wants dead. He'll definitely kill me before my mum, because I'm getting older, I'm understanding that what he is doing is wrong and I'm becoming a liability.

Not knowing how to respond to what Mr. Brown has told me, and feeling relief that it wasn't my job on the line, I pick up my bag and leave the shop to meet Earl who is waiting at the corner. He takes the bag from me without a word and wanders off. Instead of going directly to the Children's home, I take a detour past Tim's house. Everything looks the same except for the police tape on the fence and the front door. I can imagine what went on inside, even though, from the outside it looks like all the other houses.

Arriving at the Home, I knock on the door.

The Horrid Cow social worker answers. Everyone hates it when she's working; she watches us like a hawk. She sticks to all of the rules never giving anyone any leeway.

Stepping through her isn't an option, so I ask as politely as I can, "Is Doris in?"

"No."

"Do you know where she is or when she'll be back?"

"She's at a meeting with her social worker. Come back in an hour."

"Can I come in and wait?"

"No," she replies, like she's God and closes the door.

"Fucking bitch," I mutter, as I walk back along the driveway contemplating where to go now. It's no good going to Tex's; he'll still be at work. Stones fire in all directions from the toes of my shoes. I don't have that much time left. Richard will be back tomorrow.

Distracted by a tapping on glass, I look up and see Dan at his bedroom window waving and pointing to the garden door next to the garage. Ha, I'm in luck. I push my bike to the garden door and wait. It opens and Dan appears with a big, cheeky grin on his fat, rosy face.

"Quick, shhh!" He stands to the side and I sneak in, lean my bike against the wall and follow him into the back garden. We duck at the windows and scamper along past the back of the building to a fire escape door that he's left ajar. We enter, sneak up the stairs, along a corridor and through a door into his bedroom. We're both sniggering as quietly as we can. It is really scary, but exciting, knowing that the Horrid Cow is on duty somewhere. He shuts the door and puts a chair under the handle. He pushes me onto the bed and fucks me while I ask questions about the model aeroplanes hanging from his ceiling. Well, it might be useful to know the names of some of them in case the man in the glue shop ever does ask me what sort of an aeroplane I am building.

"That's a Lancaster bomber."

"And that one?"

"A Messerschmitt me 163 komet."

"And that one?"

"A Mosquito and the next is a Bristol Beaufighter." His breathing is becoming laboured, but I'm interested.

"What's the one that looks like two planes glued together?"

"It's a… Lockheed P-38 Lightning… that's my favourite." He's finished and I pull my trousers back up.

"And the last one?"

He catches his breath and lies like a star on the bed. "Supermarine Spitfire."

The 'Spitfire' sounds really hateful - I like that. Now that I know something about it, I will tell the man in the glue shop that I need the glue to build my Spitfire.

"I have to go Dan."

"Did you know that the first Spitfire prototype took off in 1936 and was piloted my Mutt Summers?"

"No. Thanks but I've gotta go."

"I've got a helicopter. It's remote control."

"Really?" I move the chair aside, and make a run for it. If the Horrid Cow spots me, I know she won't catch me - she's too fat. Down the stairs, through the garden and I'm free. As I ride to the park, I imagine I'm flying a helicopter. It must be like riding a bike except you can go up and down as well. It is added to my list of things I'm going to do when I'm a grown up.

What little time I have left, I must make the most of, for that bastard Richard will be back tomorrow evening, and I will never see the park again. It won't be worth risking going there once he's back. I'll be grounded, fucked and tortured to death if I get caught. All my hard work will have been for nothing. Fingers crossed though, he might have a serious car accident on the way home that leaves him paralysed.

I fly through in my imaginary helicopter. I'm sure it's faster than I have ever ridden. At the lake I spot my fisherman friend. He's sitting close by another fisherman. I pull up behind him.

"Have you caught anything?"

"Not yet. I've only just set up." A big shiny, white smile spreads across his face.

The other fisherman calls over, "It's amazing what you get to catch around here, eh Dave?" He starts laughing.

Now I remember his name. Dave. He had told me at some point, but I'd forgotten. I really should try and make a point of remembering it. I ignore the jibes.

"Dave, I can't come to the park anymore, but you can find me outside the girls' school at lunchtimes. Only if you want. I have to go; bye." It's a waste of a dilution, but I'm not having him fuck me with that other guy watching. I do have some decency. Dave is looking confused, but he waves goodbye. As I pass the other fisherman, I get whistled at - I give him a grimacing stare for ruining my mission. "Twat!"

Once out of view of the two of them, I ride into the back of the spinney, get off my bike and push it through the bushes until I reach the big, fallen tree log. A voice is close by, or maybe it's in my head. I can't see anybody. It seems to be coming from behind the tree log. I can't believe that it's the hippy bush because I haven't had any glue. It does sound familiar though. Resting my bike against the log, I climb up and peer over the edge. It is Pat. He is sitting on the ground between the log and the hippie bush. He is chatting away about something, but I can't understand a word of it. He has a glue bag in one hand and is pointing at the bush as he speaks.

Unable to resist, I stretch down and slap the top of his skinhead. He raises his head slowly, focuses on me, holds up the bag to me and turns back to whoever he'd been talking to. Grabbing the bag from his hand, I see a giant pot of glue by his side. This YTS thing is great. Pat looks all around for whoever he was talking to before staring at his empty hand. I jump down next to him to save him the confusion.

Kissing the bag and inhaling the fumes is dangerous. I might lose all track of time, but I haven't got long left. It's my last day and I'm determined to make the most of it.

The fumes warm me, but as I begin to relax Pat is up on his feet and pulling at my arm.

"What's the matter with you?" I say pulling away. He keeps pulling and pointing. His face is bewildered and excited, but no words are coming out of his mouth, only dribble. He snatches the bag from me and stuffs it into the pocket of his pilot jacket. He pulls at me again.

"Alright I'll come with you. Let me get my bike."

We make our way out of the spinney and across the park. I know it must look like Pat dragging me and me pulling my bike, but we are actually floating. We reach the doors of the old museum. They are open for the first time in years. He walks in through the huge doors. I stop causing him to panic. "My bike?"

He shrugs and carries on, so I follow with my bike. There doesn't seem to be anyone around. Pat continues through the museum and up a huge staircase. My bike should be safe here; I lean it against the wall at the bottom of the staircase and follow him. It is so strange in here. The place has been closed for years, but I do remember coming here as a very small child. I'm sure it was much bigger then. It's funny how things change in size as we grow. I wonder if Richard will look really small when I'm grown up.

Pat hasn't lived in this area very long so he won't have been here as a child. No wonder he looks so baffled by it all. He pauses in a corridor. A look of terror appears on his face. He grabs my arm again and leads me up a little staircase and through a door. His hand is gripping me tighter passing on the trembling of his whole body. I don't know if he's excited or scared. I'm not either; the place is familiar to me.

Entering the room he stops dead, his eyes widen as he looks around then back to me.

The room contains many large, glass cabinets housing a variety of stuffed animals, mainly birds. They're the same ones that I'd seen as a little child. They are crude and tatty.

Pointing to a stuffed fox I laugh. "Either, the guy that stuffed that was sick, or it was one hell of a cross-eyed fox when it was alive."

"Shhh." Pat seems to be utterly amazed by the sight.

"What's wrong?"

"They're all fucking dead and they're all fucking staring at me." He reaches out with both arms and presses them against the glass. He stares into the fox's crossed-eyes.

"They're just all dead. They're not staring at you and they can't see you."

"How do you know?" He puts his hand on his crotch and turns to me.

"Because! What's wrong with you?"

"Nothing, come here." He takes my arm and pulls me around the side of a huge glass cabinet containing two Bewick swans posing on a nest of eggs. He undoes his jeans and fucks me really quick against the cabinet. So quick that I just have time to read the information card on Bewick swans.

Their Latin name is Cygnus Columbianus. I must remember that. Every eye in the room is watching us, but nothing stirs. Pat seems to have got some weird kick out of fucking me in front of all the dead things, with all their beady glass eyes on us. He does his trousers up and shudders as we leave the room. I'm not complaining; I've diluted Richard a bit more. This week I have really accomplished something. My bike is still safe at the bottom of the stairs.

"Do you want a backie to the Home? I've gotta meet my brother." Earl is sure to be finished the round by now.

"OK." Pat climbs onto the saddle. I ride back through the park and past the lake. A swan is being fed near the edge by two children.

Pat cries out to it, "I send you love from your great, great grandfather." Boys can be so stupid sometimes. If he'd read the card in the museum, he'd realise he wasn't shouting at a Bewick swan but a Mute swan.

I drop Pat at the alley behind the home. He's not finished sniffing and knows that the Horrid Cow is on duty. I check the purple bush, but my bag's not in it. I spot Earl turning the corner. What excellent timing.

Doris comes running out of the Home. Her face is red with rage. She storms towards me and slaps me hard across the face.

"That's for having sex with my boyfriend, bitch." She marches back to the home and stands in the doorway. Dan appears and puts his arm around her and grins. I want to scream an explanation. I didn't know they'd got together, but fuck it, I don't particularly care. Mission complete.

Earl hands me the bag and says nothing about the scene he's just witnessed. "When do I get paid?"

My face is stinging. "Tomorrow, when I do. Bugger off."

I return the bag to the shop before going home - home for the last time without Richard being there. I'm not going to think about tomorrow. I know tomorrow is going to be hell, but that's tomorrow.

I go straight to my room and sit in the wardrobe. The silverfish have multiplied, and are taking up a large section of one wall. I mess with them, disrupting their colony and watch them shimmer as they try to reorganise themselves, over and over again, until I crawl to bed and my last decent night's sleep.

Because you're Young
Friday.

I wake several times during the night. Jolted from my sleep by monsters and silverfish. I would rather die than see this day.

I leave the house and my numbness returns. Mr. Brown has found someone to do Tim's round, so I have to do mine really slowly. I need to keep time consistency. It seemed like a good idea to have the extra time for myself, but no one will want me bothering them at this time in the morning. Tex might be up getting ready for work, but he's probably rushing about, and wouldn't appreciate a visitor. All I can do is take my time. It's really quite pointless wandering between the houses with my bike. I reassure myself that I might need this extra time one day, and then I'll be glad of it.

A huge pressure is squeezing my head. Each step I take, each paper I deliver brings me closer to Richard's return. Why can't time stop? Why can't it always be yesterday? I'm getting wet. I hadn't even noticed it is raining - it's pissing me off. Maybe it's not the rain. It doesn't usually bother me. No, I'm pissed off because Richard will be back this evening. Back to fuck with my mind and my body. The annoyance and fear of impending danger is also pissing me off, because he won't be home until this evening. I should be enjoying my last hours of freedom. I haven't felt that I'm standing on a cliff top on a windy day all week. It's back now - it's back to stay until the day I'm old enough to get away. Even that description is not strong enough for how I feel right now. The fear, the helplessness, the frustration, the anger and the hatefulness can't match any situation I have ever encountered.

The round finished, I head off towards school. I am so angry. I want to beat the shit out of someone. I know it's nobody else's fault, and no one deserves my wrath except Richard. What pisses me off even more is that I'm not big enough to beat the fucking shit out of him. Even if I had enough money to pay someone to beat the shit out of him, he would know it was something to do with me, and then he'd make my mum's life hell. My brother and sister would suffer even more and he'd … well … kill me.

I had turned around to him once, when I was younger and braver, on leaving his room and told him that I would kill him one day. He told me in his nasally, evil, best horror movie voice that I'd never get the chance to kill him because he would kill me first, and if for any reason he died before me, that he would haunt and fuck me until I went mad and killed myself. I've never mentioned it to him again, but I still mean it.

I want to believe in God when Richard says stuff like that to me. At least then, if we both die, I'd know that he'll be in Hell and I'll be in heaven. It would be worth it, as we'd never be in the same place ever again. I can't believe in God though; it doesn't make sense. Why is my life so hellish if there is a God? Why does he make me go through this shit? It has been like this all of my life that I can remember. Is this it? Is this how it's always going to be? Surely one day it has to end; somehow it has to. If only I knew the ending, like a film, I could stop it sooner, but I am too scared, too small and there are other people to consider. It's not fair.

I arrive at my school early. It's pointless wandering and wondering in the rain. I can dry off in the bike sheds while I wait for Jane, I don't have a bike lock and since the first day of school, when I told her to lock my bike with hers, she has continued to do so every day since.

She arrives bang on time - swotty cow. She's never late or misses a day. She locks my bike with hers without speaking to me. I leave her to it.

First lesson is Maths. I find Maths really easy, but they've put me in the thick class because I'm disruptive - bored more like.

Trying not to think about the evening ahead is difficult, but I'm sitting next to Punjit, and she's crap at Maths. I can't understand why, as she speaks perfect English, like the queen, even though her family can't speak a word. She learnt the language within a year of coming to England, so she must be clever.

We have to share a text book because there is a shortage of everything. The book looks fifty years old, but as Maths stays the same (unlike history) it doesn't really matter. She is absolutely rubbish at maths though.

Today's page numbers are scrawled on the blackboard. The teacher doesn't even speak to us. He's doing something else at his desk. Our task is to write down the answers, including our workings out, from the appropriate pages and leave them on his desk at the end of the lesson. Simple, but boring and what have we learnt? Zilch!

Looking at the first page, I decide it's a waste of time. I can work out the answers in my head. It isn't worth writing anything. The same with the next page. Punjit stops me. "I haven't finished that page."

"Look, that's 396, and that's 26.25, that's…"

"There is no point in you telling me the answers if I don't understand how you came to the conclusion."

Isn't it the teacher's job to explain and teach us how to do Maths? He's engrossed in something, so I spend the lesson teaching Punjit the basics of Mathematics, and she picks it up really quickly. I knew she wasn't thick.

Punjit happily hands her papers onto the teacher's desk. I don't bother. I haven't written anything, and I'm saving him some marking. I think he appreciates it, as he's never punished me, or even mentioned the fact that I never hand anything in. I don't think he gives a shit. I wonder why he decided to become a teacher in the first place. He's probably very disillusioned, and it must be frustrating trying to teach the thick group.

At lunchtime, I go out to the front of the school in the hope that Dave turns up. I don't think he will, and I can't see anyone around that looks like him. As he isn't going to be sitting under a fishing umbrella, or in a bush with his trousers down, I wonder if I'd even recognise him. He had looked a little shocked when I'd said 'school', he must have thought I was older. Never mind, but it would have been handy for my chart.

Instead of hanging about, I cross the road to the shop. Doris and some other girls, from her class, are leaning against the shop front sharing a fag. She sticks her nose up in the air, sniffs and marches off. The other girls follow her. A shrill beeping of a horn makes everyone jump, as a car brakes hard outside the shop. I glare at the car. I am pissed off enough without some twat scaring the living daylights out of me, today of all days.

I recognise the driver. Dave is leaning out of the window beckoning me to the yellow Capri with a black material roof. I relax, smile, and walk towards the car. Jeers of 'slag' and 'cocksucker' are yelled by Doris and her friends. This really pisses me off, as I have never sucked anyone's cock. That is my only virginity. I'm saving it for the right person one day - maybe even until I'm married. Even Richard cannot force that on me. My teeth are always clenched. My gums, lips and teeth might feel that grotesque, stinking skin trying to get in, but my teeth stay tightly shut. I think Richard worries that, if he ever did get in, I would bite his stinking, skinny cock off.

I jump into Dave's car and fling my arms around him. He pushes me off. "What's with the uniform? I thought you must be in the sixth form. How old are you?"

"I'm sixteen. My birthday was last week. If I'd been born two weeks earlier, I would be in the sixth form." It is half true, and I'm not going to ruin this opportunity by telling him I'm only fourteen.

The girls are still pointing and jeering at me.

"Please drive somewhere."

He drives somewhere - somewhere I've never been or seen before. I am so relaxed, and watching the clouds, that I don't even know which direction we've taken. This isn't like me at all; I'm usually highly aware of everything that is going on. I wish he would just keep driving and never stop, but he parks up in an isolated place in the woods. I've never been here before, but I'm not scared. I wish I could stay here with him forever. He fucks me on the back seat of the car while I ask him questions.

"How old are you then?"

"I'm nearly twenty."

"Is this your car?"

"Yes."

"Do you have a girlfriend?"

"Yes. I don't know why though."

"Will you come and see me next week, at lunchtime?"

"Yes … yes … yes."

I like him and I believe him - he's very honest.

He drops me back at school. "See ya soon."

I don't go to my English lesson. Instead I sit in the toilets with some sixth-form smokers, and listen to them chatting about hairdressers. My English teacher told me weeks ago that I am a distraction to her, and she'd rather I didn't turn up at all. It's fine by me. It seems that most of the kids want to learn, but the teachers aren't capable of teaching. I'm her scapegoat; it's my fault that her class isn't learning or passing anything. I'm used to it; everything is my fault. It always has been and it always will be.

One girl offers me a fag.

"No thanks. I don't smoke."

"You have to start sometime - have one."

I shake my head; I don't want to. I know how it feels to have to share a small amount of glue with five people. To get hooked on cigarettes, and be in the same position would piss me off. Selfish I know, but true. There is also the fear that Richard would smell the smoke and have another reason to punish me. He must be able to smell the glue, but he never mentions it. I think it's because a lot of kids have been found dead recently with glue bags stuck in their throats, or they've jumped off buildings believing they can fly. That's why he doesn't say anything. He's hoping it happens to me.

"Be like that then." They carry on their conversation.

Last lesson is judo; I love judo. Although it's called judo, and the teacher is a real judo instructor in a judo suit, he is really teaching us self-defence and moves that will help us if someone tries to attack us. His name is Stan and he always picks me to demonstrate throwing and holding techniques. I think he's comfortable about throwing me around, holding me down and getting me in locks. He must sense that I am used to it. It could be that some of the other girls would cry, but I believe that he knows there is an urgency for me to learn to defend myself. Whatever he thinks, he never says anything rude or suggestive to me. He never has a hard on when he is lying on top of me with his arm across my throat, and my arms pinned above my head. I like Stan; he has taught me some good moves, and I'm pretty strong from all the cycling as well. I am getting bigger, stronger and I yearn for more.

After the instruction, we get to play a game on the mats. The rules are simple. The last one left on the mat is the winner. I think some of the girls pretend to get thrown off on purpose before I can get near them. Others are as enthusiastic as me; I wonder if they are angry about something too. We have a real good wrestle, and even though we're not allowed to fight, only practise the moves, hair pulling and biting has been known. It's the perfect way to end the day, today anyway.

I leave the school day behind me and ride to the shop. My bigness leaves me. I will be brought back down to size very soon.

I meet Earl and make up a story. "I got out of school early today. I've already done my half, so I'll give you a hand."

"Okay."

I don't know if Richard is home yet or not. I can't risk getting caught straight away. If he's watching me, it'll look like Earl is helping me. I have to keep one step ahead.

Neither of us mention Richard. We don't speak at all during the round, or on the slow journey home. We walk into the house together in silence. I lean my bike against the wall beneath the 'clocking-in' clock. Richard is standing at the bottom of the stairs. His hands are behind his back and he's rocking back and forth on his heels. My mum is pretending to be doing something in the kitchen, but I can see her head sticking out from the door under the giant clock with no body. She looks anxious.

Richard grabs Earl by his shirt collar and throws him into the front room, he follows and slams the door behind him. My mum clatters something in the kitchen. I stand and wait. I don't know what Earl has done wrong - probably nothing. I can hear Richard's voice. It gets even more nasal as he screams. I'm listening hard for a clue, but I'm no wiser to what Earl has done wrong. I can hear the insults. They are long words for 'stupid'. With each insult there is a thud or a crash. I know it's Earls body bouncing off walls and furniture. I still stand waiting. I'm too scared to move because that would make things worse - worse for everybody.

The door swings open. Earl walks out, heading towards the stairs, the way he's been told to. His eyes are full of tears and hate, but he doesn't look at me. He runs up the stairs stamping his feet down as hard as he can. He lets out a scream, not in the way that he's been told to.

Richard runs after him screaming in a ridiculously high pitched voice. He chases Earl up the stairs. He could have caught Earl by the seventh step, but he doesn't. As Earl is one stair from the top, Richard grabs him by one ankle, then by the other. He pulls Earl all the way back down the stairs - hitting his head on the stairs, the banister and the walls. Throughout it all Richard continues to scream wild words that only mad people would understand. Earl isn't giving in lightly. His face is so red with anger it looks like it could explode. He thrashes his body and screams as loud as Richard. My ears can't take the mixture of high frequency, and the sound distorts to a herd of whale songs. It is only disturbed by the odd crash from the kitchen.

I stand rigid on the spot where I first entered the house. If I move the attention will be turned to me. I want to help Earl and I want to run away, but I'll only make matters worse if I do.

Earl goes silent - he's being held by the throat.

"From now on, you will be doing the whole paper round. You will get all the money. Do you hear me you imbecile?"

Earl is being held so hard that he can't answer or nod. Richard throws him onto the stairs. "Get out of my sight you cretin."

This time, without stamping or screaming, Earl walks up the stairs. I doubt he's got any energy left. I wonder who has told Richard about Earl doing my round. I know how crafty Richard is. It's probably a trick. It's what he would have expected me to do, and he's calling my bluff.

I swallow and await my turn.

Richard steps towards me. I stand firm, but I don't make eye contact. His body is still shaking with the rage. He pokes his finger into my shoulder, just below my collar bone, again and again, harder and harder. He's trying to push me off the spot that I'm fixed to. He's trying to force me to step back. I take each poke, I sway, but I stay on the spot.

"And what have you got to say for yourself. You scraggy little nutrag."

I know I should answer something. He commands an answer. I try to think of something that will appease him, but I haven't got a clue what he wants me to say. I know he wants me to admit to something, so he can punish me, but what? He's done this before, this reverse psychology, I'm not falling for it again. If I knew what he knows, I'd admit to it, but I'm not giving him the ammunition. It crosses my mind that maybe he hasn't been away for a week. Maybe he's been following me. I dismiss the thought, knowing that he wouldn't have taken so long to find a reason for punishing me.

I shrug my shoulders and try to look confused. Something else clatters in the kitchen; it's like a cue for me to say something. Something that will please him and end the charade.

He stops poking me, and his face closes in an inch from mine. The clocking-in clock is ticking loudly in my right ear. I count the seconds going by in my head. I imagine that I'm not here. My eyes are drawn to the floor. A wood louse is trying hard to negotiate the bristle doormat. It struggles to climb the edge of bristles and falls on its back. I can feel Richard's breath on my face, but I concentrate my thoughts on the wood louse. It is determined to get up and over the mat. It tries several times until it makes it. It runs the width of the mat and disappears under the front door. I can't blame it for wanting to get out of this fucking house. I so wish I was that wood louse at this moment.

"Go to your room and have a think - you scrag end. I'll be up shortly and you better have some answers."

I do as I'm told. I know it's not answers he wants.

My little sister is sitting on the floor, between our beds, playing with little people in a shoe box. She doesn't even acknowledge me. I pick up a book and sit in the wardrobe, but I don't read. I wait. I can hear Richard raging at my mum in the kitchen below. She's getting called all the other insults that he knows. She'll be going to work soon and it'll be my turn.

I don't hear Richard come up the stairs, but I hear him in Earl's room, so I sit on my bed and start reading. He enters my room, and ignoring me, he speaks to my sister. "You're tea's on the table." She gets up without a word and leaves the room. He follows her slamming the door behind him.

I wonder how often my mum must buy new plates - I wait. The front door shuts; my mum has gone to work. Within seconds Richard is in my room and gives me the punishment that he believes I deserve. I know nothing of it though; I have already curled up into a small place in the back of my head where he can't get to me.

My mum is only gone for two hours. She does something at an old people's home. When she walks in, Richard gathers us altogether in the living room.

"During my absence it has become apparent that things have gone a little astray around here, to put it mildly. To get things back on track, you are all grounded until further notIce."

I can't say I wasn't expecting it because I was. I know how this twat's mind works. Earl looks shocked though, as he's never been grounded no matter what he's done. He gets battered around as his punishment. Richard encourages him to be out of the house as much as possible, probably so he can punish me in peace.

My little sister only ever goes to her friend's

house across the street. I can't see why she deserves to be grounded. I try to figure what his game is. My sister starts to cry.

"Why are you crying, you baby?"

" 'Cos I can't go to Polly's house anymore."

"You can go to Polly's house, but that's it. I'll know where you are. That's different."

She stops crying.

This is all so pathetic. The twat realises he's losing his authority as we get older, and believes that imprisoning us is the answer. He's been away for five days and we've all seen how much better it is without him around. I think even Earl might be contemplating killing him. I can't risk mentioning it to him though. I want to come up with a plan to kill him, but I don't want to spend twenty-five years in jail. I've only a few more years of putting up with this. Years, God that is such a depressing thought, but not as bad as life in jail for murder. I'd have no future at all. I must be sensible - I must hold it together for a little while longer.

Earl coughs. "Please may I use the telephone?"

"What for?"

"I told Luke that I'd go fishing with him tomorrow morning. I said I'd call for him at eight."

"You can go fishing. I'm talking about hanging around streets. You can go fishing and you can do the evening paper round, but that's it. I want you in this house at all other times."

I'm horrified, and blurt out without thinking.

"But he's only ten. He's not old enough to do a paper round."

"I have already informed Mr. Brown that you are grounded and why. He is happy to let Earl continue with the round until such time that I feel fit. He's already lost a paper boy this week."

I wonder what reason, why, he has told Mr. Brown. It'll be a pack of lies whatever it is. "What about my morning round?"

"You can still do your morning round, but that's it. Studying for your exams is what you should be concentrating your energies on."

I try to figure it out. We've all been grounded, but we've all been given some leeway. Is he trying to look fair in front of my mum? No. She'd agree with whatever he decided. It doesn't seem very fair though. My sister is allowed to go to the only place she ever goes to anyway, and I'm sure Earl has figured out that, as long as he takes his fishing kit with him, he is free to do what he likes. I, on the other hand, am a prisoner. I wonder how long for. If I don't ask, I won't know and that will be torturous. If I do ask, it'll be seen as insolence and will be extended. What am I thinking? It will be extended anyway. Forever.

"How long am I grounded for?"

"Until I tell you...you're not. Now go to your rooms."

Scary Monsters
Saturday.

I can't believe Richard came and bothered me again last night. I pretended to be asleep. It will annoy him that I didn't notice his punishment. I didn't sleep well, but I still get up on time to do my round. I need to get out of this house; I need to get out of it forever.

As I walk down the stairs, Earl passes through the hall to the front door with his fishing kit.

Trying not to wake anyone, I ask, "Are you still going fishing? It's pouring down out there."

"Yes. I'm going fishing every day. All day." Although he says it seriously, he has a devilish smirk on his face. I can't blame him. If I was allowed to go fishing I'd do the same. This reminds me of a wildlife program I once saw. The younger monkeys were trying to outfox the Alpha male. They snuck behind his back and did things he wouldn't approve of. The Alpha male would sometimes catch them and beat the shit out of them to take control of his status, and so the cycle continued until a younger monkey was big enough to win the fight. There is hope for us yet.

Earl rushes through the front door at the sound of footsteps on the landing. I attempt to follow him, but a voice stops me in my tracks. "Wait."

Richard is fully clothed and putting his coat on. He must have stayed up all night. I freeze and wait as he descends the stairs doing up his coat buttons.

"You can't go riding around in this weather you'll get soaked. I'll drive you. Come on."

I can't speak. My heart sinks into my stomach. I follow him to the car and become a zombie - the zombie he has made me.

I'm unaware of the drive to the shop. I collect my bag without speaking to Mr. Brown. I get back in the car knowing that this journey is a test. A time test. I'm going to get as wet running back and forth to the car, as I would have on my bike. He's working out how long the round should take me. Where I will be at any particular moment and putting pressure on me to be punctual. I'll have no time for myself. I am now a true prisoner.

I deliver the last paper and expect that we'll drive back to the shop. Richard has something else in mind. He drives in the opposite direction and out of town. I don't question it. I don't speak at all; I'm not here. I stare ahead - still a zombie. He pulls over into a gateway of a cow field. It is light now, but the sky is grey and it's still raining hard.

He leans over me and takes a newspaper out of the glove compartment. It's slapped down on my lap.

"Read it."

It's a copy of our local evening newspaper, but it's over a year old. I start to read the front page headline story. It is about a newspaper boy who had been horribly murdered in one of the alleys - two streets away from our house. I can remember hearing about it, but I didn't know him, so I hadn't taken much notice at the time.

I finish reading the article and pass the paper back to Richard. I keep a blank face; I'm not going to look scared. I want to say 'Yeah, and?' but I'm afraid he'll attack me for being cheeky.

"The killer has never been caught. There is someone out there still - who murders paperboys and girls - I assume. Next time it could be you." He snatches the newspaper from me and stuffs it back into the glove compartment. He pulls out of the gateway and we head back to the shop. He drives really fast, stupidly fast, skidding around corners and laughing like a fucking lunatic. I ignore his attempts at trying to scare the life out of me. I wonder whether he was trying to tell me that he'd killed the boy, or if he is going to kill me one morning, leaving the blame on the killer at large. Whatever he is plotting, I'm not afraid. I'm in serious danger though, and I come to the conclusion that enough is enough; I have to get out of here no matter what trouble it causes.

I spend the afternoon listening to music and pretending to read in my room. I'm not concerned about the paper boy. What is troubling me more, is that Richard has kept that newspaper for over a year. Surely he doesn't plan that far ahead. Either he kept it because he killed the boy, or he knew that one day I'd get a paper round and he could use it to scare the shit out of me. Trying to stay one step ahead of him is impossible if he's a whole year ahead of me in his schemes.

"And Tim. What did Tim do wrong to get his mother murdered?"

'Oh and now you're back. What are you trying to say? That Tim's mum got murdered because he did something wrong. I was thinking of running away, but I know Richard will take it out on my mum and Earl. It's me he wants to kill though. Is it worth the risk of waiting to be grown up? I might never get to be grown up.'

Retreating to the wardrobe to escape the voice doesn't work.

"Why do you insist on sitting in here with those things crawling all over the wall?"

'Well, it's not because I'm insecure or crazy or agoraphobic. It's because of Richard's weirdness. He watches through keyholes, cracks in doors, floorboards and ceilings. He has strategically placed mirrors around the house, so that even from downstairs he can see upstairs into rooms. He watches us through them and sometimes I get a glimpse of him doing something very odd somewhere in the house. I know he does it on purpose. It wouldn't surprise me if there are hidden cameras everywhere too. I've checked the wardrobe though. There are no cameras and I'm out of view of his mirrors. In here it's only me and the silverfish.'

I can smell myself. I can smell the damp on the wall where the silverfish live, but they're good.

They eat the mould and keep me company.

"Why don't you have a bath if you smell?"

'I can't remember the last time I had a bath. I pretend to. I run it, stay dressed and wet my hair because I know he's watching me from somewhere. Go away now - I need the toilet, and I can't even do that in peace. This is shit - I always go to the toilet somewhere else, but now I'm grounded I'm gonna have to put up with that old routine too.'

"What's that supposed to mean?"

'Please go away now.'

Creeping from my room to the toilet without treading on any creaky boards is difficult, but doable with practice. Locking the door in silence is impossible though, and within seconds Richard's voice is on the other side of the door.

"That poo looks like it'll stink. You want to open the window. You'll be in there a long while. Don't open the door and let your shit stink out into my house you stinking, filthy rag. Talking of rags - on blob week make sure you don't flush them down the toilet; else you'll be unblocking the drains. I'm not going down there with all your germs and diseases."

I don't reply. I have a little dream in my head about the future, my dreams and goals. There are fewer years of this life in front of me than there are behind me. In the future I will have escaped this hellhole. I'll meet a nice man and live in a nice house and have some babies; babies that are loved and love me back. No one is going to be horrid. I won't tolerate any mad fuckers in my happy house. I have a picture of my wonderful husband in my head. I will find him one day. I will paint that grandfather clock pink. I will paint the sundial with stripes, but I've decided I no longer want to buy that house; I want to be as far away from here as possible. I'm going to fly a helicopter; the traffic is bad enough now, so in the future I will need a helicopter. I also want to say thank you to David Bowie because his songs have helped me through some bad feelings.

'Really. Thank you.'

I pause my thoughts at the sound of the voice. I wait for more, but nothing comes. I knew it. I knew I recognised that voice. It's David Bowie. I don't know how he does it, but I know it's him.

Richard might have left, or he might still be behind the door watching me. I don't care. David Bowie is going to make sure everything's fine. I flush the toilet and exit. Richard is standing on the landing with his hands behind his back. No one else is home. He lunges towards me, pushes me back into the bathroom and locks the door.

I switch off.

Starman
Sunday.

I don't get a lift to do my round this morning, although it is still pissing down with rain. Richard has what he wants - a time scale to punish me. Earl is up having breakfast. I pass his fishing kit awaiting him in the hallway. This round is no fun anymore. I have no time and I can't even spend what I earn. My life is now pointless. Richard will easily be top of the dilution tables again soon. All my hard work has been ripped like a rug from under my feet.

I rush the paper round hoping to gain myself some time, but it's only a matter of minutes I save. Opening the porch door at the final house, I notice a letter stuck to the door addressed to 'Paper boy'.

Shoving the newspaper and supplements through the small letterbox one at a time, I wonder if there could be a tip in the envelope. I tear it down and open it. There's no tip.

'To Brown's Newsagent's newspaper boy.

While being a loyal and valued customer of Mr. Brown's newsagents, I have appreciated the regularity of my morning newspaper to arrive before seven thirty of a morning. Sadly it seems that this week things have changed without me being given prior warning. I find this, regretfully, insulting. If my newspaper cannot arrive before seven thirty in the future, I shall have no choice but to take my custom elsewhere.

Regards,
Mr. Richards.'

I am devastated by his words. If I change the round back to how it was originally, I'll be late. If I keep it how it is, Mr. Brown will lose a customer and he'll find out why. I'll get the sack and be a complete prisoner. Riding back to the shop I'm vexed that the man is also called Richard – well, Mr. Richards, same thing. All Richards must have it in for me. All Richards are evil. My anger getting the better of me, I decide to continue to do the job the way Mr. Richards wants it. I will steal his milk checks and his bills from his porch and drop them down a drain. The bailiffs will empty his house and he might end up in court. It'll serve him right for the shit I'm going to get for being late.

I storm into the shop and throw my bag down on the floor. "Change the route back to how it was," I shout at Mr. Brown. He looks surprised by my uncharacteristic outburst. His head wobbles. "Okay. Is every..."

I'm out of the shop before he can finish. I ride home with my hands clenched so tight that my knuckles have gone white. I've had enough. I have to get away from all this, but I need a plan.

Back at the house the usual Sunday ritual transpires - the only digression is the absence of Earl. I wonder why Richard has allowed him to go fishing on a Sunday. I give up wondering. I have something else on my mind - my escape.

Earl returns home within minutes of Uncle's

family arriving, the lucky boy, he's not half as stupid as Richard thinks.

The adults drink beer in the living room and talk about politics and investments. I am left to entertain the kids. I make them drinks in the kitchen, but I'm distracted by the cordial bottle. I pour a drop of lime into a glass, add water and taste it. I add more water and taste it again. I add even more so it overflows into the sink, and I taste it again. It can be diluted away. The drink no longer tastes of lime. The liquid is clear, but five thirsty faces are staring at me in bewilderment.

I tip it away and make the drinks properly. I'm happy; I've proved I can dilute Richard to nothing if only I can get out of here.

I take the kids up to my room and play a cassette that I recorded from the radio. I make them all look up at the sky through my sealed window, and I tell them a story about a Starman in space who comes to visit me. Earl isn't impressed and goes to his room, but the little ones look and listen in wonderment. Why they look up to me, I do not know.

When they leave I'm alone again. My sister went to bed and is already asleep. I can tell because I can hear her sucking her fingers. It sounds like she's sucking the last remaining drops of a milkshake through a straw. Two of her fingers are now deformed, bent inwards and backwards due to this habit. I've heard that if sucking habits continue past the age of seven - then you're stuck with it forever. I wonder if her future husband will be able to tolerate the constant snorking noises.

Lying on my bed with a book strategically placed on my chest. I consider my options of escape. I can't get out of the house during the night, as I would make too much noise. I'd have to remove the screws in the window first, and it would be impossible to open it without making a sound. The front and back door aren't an option, as the bolts are big and heavy. I doubt I'd even make it down the stairs without being heard.

School or paper round? If I don't turn up for the round Mr. Brown will phone and Richard will be on my tail in no time. Mr. Brown said he'd tried to ring Tim when he hadn't turned up. Hmm Tim; I try not to think about him and the murder of his mother. If my mum gets murdered then it's her own stupid fault for not leaving the nutcase. I've done everything I can to keep the peace, but it's pointless. I'm not putting up with it anymore. I can't - I want to live.

It's going to have to be before school. I can catch a train and be far away before anyone notices I'm missing. I'm going to need money, at least a hundred pounds. If I save my paper round money and whatever I get in Christmas tips, I should have a hundred pounds by the New Year. It'll be cold, but what a great time to start a new life. New year it is. That's just over three months. I can tolerate this for three months knowing that I'll be free. I'll catch the train to London. I can disappear amongst the crowds. I'll change my appearance. He'll never find me.

"Do you know anyone in London?"

'No I don't. Not yet. I've heard stories of people going there, sleeping in the streets and becoming prostitutes. So fucking what if I become a prostitute? At least I'll be getting paid for it.'

Bowie doesn't respond. I'm getting used to that. My bedroom door opens. I raise the book above my face and pretend to be reading. "Come and help me put the rubbish out you lazy cretin."

I follow Richard in silence down the stairs and through the back door. We each pick up two black bin bags, walk up the garden path, go through the garage into the alley and drop them there before re-entering the garage. I have already escaped to the back of my head where London is waiting for me.

Station to Station
Three months later.

I nearly didn't make it, but I have. Tomorrow will be the beginning of the rest of my life. I really don't care what happens in this house after I'm gone. I hope things will get better for everyone. With me out of the way, Richard might not be so stressed.

I haven't succeeded with my dilution experiment. I've stopped filling in the graph because it's too painful to see my efforts quashed and insignificant. I haven't had a chance to visit Tex. Dave hasn't turned up at lunchtime since his shock of seeing me in uniform. Even if he had, I have to report to reception twice at lunchtime on Richard's orders to my school. I don't know what he's told them, but it must be bad, as they'll call him if I don't report in. Doris still isn't talking to me. She has a new best mate. The pair of them snub me or call me names. I heard Pat died; he fell of a roof on the YTS. He was probably high on glue, but nobody told me at the time. I would have liked to have gone to the funeral. Maybe that's why he was so fascinated by the dead creatures in the museum - being that close to his own death. My bike got stolen a couple of weeks ago. Earl was using it to do the paper round. He'd only popped in the shop to pick up the paper bag. He said it vanished in seconds and he couldn't see anyone riding away. It must have been thrown into a car and my bet is on

Richard. Everyone around here knows it's my bike. I'm pretty sure they wouldn't try to steal it.

That was when I got to my lowest point. My bike was gone forever and I had a particularly nasty punishment from Richard - to do with respecting property and the value of money. The two weeks' holiday from school didn't help - being trapped here throughout. I took a bottle of pills and I ate them all over Christmas. I went to sleep that night hoping to never wake up. I did wake up, and the only effect the vitamin C pills had on me was to make my piss bright orange. It also smelt of Sugar Puffs for quite a few days after. At the time I felt like a failure, but it soon became clear that my bike theft has made my escape plan much easier. I'm glad there weren't any stronger pills in the house because I'm still here, and tomorrow I will be alive and far away. My only companions have been the silverfish and David's voice in my head. Even though he is less than helpful, I hope he comes with me.

Now that I have no bike, I'll have to walk straight to school from my round or I'll be late, but I'm not intending on going to school tomorrow. It will be perfect. Richard won't know that I'm missing until four in the afternoon; I'll be long gone. I have over a hundred pounds, but no passport. It's probably a blessing. If I had a passport, I could be traced easier. Disappearing in London is the safest answer. I wish I could sleep, so the morning comes quicker, but I can't. I'm terrified and doubts are trying to make me change my mind, but I won't, I can't. I will die if I have to stay here any longer.

The stairs creak with footsteps - that will be my mum going to bed early. I don't hear the bolts on the doors locking, so that means Richard is staying up late. I hate it when my mum goes to bed first. I'll pretend I'm asleep. This will be the last time he ever touches me.

I can't sleep because I'm waiting for him. When he's gone I can't sleep for the adrenalin pumping through my head. It's over - he'll never touch me again, but it is the longest night of my life. Fear keeps me awake, but not fear of being rumbled, fear of slipping up. Something will go wrong - I know it will - it's my luck. How can I expect it to be so simple, and go so smoothly? I'm a doomed person; I always have been. I try to beat off the negative thoughts by imagining my other option. Existing in this house for a few more years isn't really an option at all. I imagine my gravestone and how I would die. Would it be my own doing? Or would it be at the hands of Richard? A body found in the alley. The verdict would be murder and the suspect would be the paperboy killer. Richard would get away with it and I'd be dead - never able to tell a soul what he'd done. He might go on to do it to other kids; a flush of guilt tells me that I'm a coward. If I run, more kids could be hurt and killed, but I can't stop that now. No one would believe me if I spoke out. I'd still have to live here until he set up a way to murder me, and I believe he already has.

My alarm clatters; I switch it off, get out of bed and put on as many layers of clothing as will fit under my uniform without making me look conspicuous. My parka conceals the lumpiness of my shape and I leave the house breathless. I pass the sundial house with a smugness that I will never see it again. My stride is strong. Outside of the house, these are my first steps to freedom, yet I am wary that eyes are watching and following my every move.

At the shop I take my bag and concentrate on acting normal. "Morning, Mr. Brown."

"Good morning, Marie. You seem rather chirpy; are you looking forward to going back to school?"

"Um, yes. I suppose," I say, immediately regretting the stupid answer.

"You're a strange one. I thought you might have bought a new bike with your Christmas tips."

"Right. They aren't that generous." I don't want to talk to him. I'm scared he'll notice that I'm being strange. I leave to do the round. I want to run it, but I must keep everything the same. I must get back to the shop at a normal time. I must make it seem like I've vanished. Apart from a few missing clothes that no one will really notice, it'll be like I've been abducted by aliens. No note, no reason to run away, no evidence that anything was planned and no confidants to grass me up. It's perfect.

At Mr. Richards' house, I'm tempted to take his mail and drop it in the drain, but it's too risky. Today would be the day that he caught me. He'd ring the police and that would fuck everything up. I'm determined I'm not going to tempt fate to get in my way. I finish the round unscathed; everything is going to plan.

I take my bag back to the shop. Mr. Brown and his wife are restocking the shelves. "See...you...tomorrow," I say, wondering what has happened to my voice.

"Marie, if you give me two minutes, I'll give you a lift to school. I have to go to the wholesaler's - I'll drop you on the way, seeing as you've lost your bike."

I can't believe what I'm hearing. For the first time in my life someone is being nice to me. Someone is trying to do me a favour and at the very worst moment they could pick. I shake my head and try to think of an excuse.

"I'll just get my coat and car keys."

I turn and leave the shop. I have to hide. I have to catch the bus to town, but Mr. Brown will see me at the bus stop. I step into a gateway of a garden and watch from behind a privet bush for Mr. Brown's car to drive away. It's an agonising wait and the bus passes by. I want to cry. I should be on that bus; the whole world is against me.

I spot Mr. Brown's car and duck behind the bush. I count to ten; he should be gone. There'll be another bus. I have to get to the bus stop. As I focus my mind to walk forward, something strange happens to my legs. They're rubbish - they won't walk properly. They've turned to rubber and I truly fear I'm going to fall over. Of all the things that could stop me catching the bus and executing my plan, the last thing I'd have expected is my own legs to fail me.

One step in front of another my legs tremble with weakness. Maybe I've put so much strength into my head to do this that there's none left to work my legs.

People must be looking at me. I need to go unnoticed, but I might as well have a huge spotlight pointing down on me. Just a few more steps. Don't give up on me legs - come on - nearly there.

I reach the bus stop, but I can't stand at it, as someone might see me. I lean against the wall away from the bus shelter with my head down. My legs give way at the knees, but I lock them to stay upright, so I don't crumple to the floor. I breathe deeply and slowly, willing blood and oxygen to my legs. I spot the bus at the end of the street. I can't move my legs. My knees touch each other and heighten the trembling as they rattle. The bus is getting closer; I have to move forward, but I can't.

I hold out my arm showing my intention. I want to cry. I've never cried in my life, as far as I recall. Right now I could drop to the floor and cry forever.

The bus pulls up at the stop. Damn it. It's not even the bus that goes straight to town. It goes all over the place before getting to town. That's the least of my worries though. I'm scared to step forward in case I collapse.

The doors open and the driver stares at me. Still I can't move. "Are you getting on or what?" he shouts at me.

I nod once. Him shouting at me raises a surge of anger - anger and energy - enough to propel me forward and onto the bus. I pay my fare and sit down. I have made another mistake. Not only have I drawn attention to myself from the driver, but all the passengers are staring at me. I tuck my head as low into my shoulders as I can be comfortable with. I don't want to be seen from the street. Anyone could see me through these big windows, and ask my mum why I was on the bus and not on my way to school. The bus drives past the bottom of the street where I live. Why won't it go any faster? This is pure agony and, so far, I'm only fifty metres from my front door.

The bus journey continues at a slow pace. We must be hitting every red light on the way, but finally everything goes dark and I'm in the bus station. I have to get through the town centre and to the train station. It's only a fifteen minute walk, but I'm not sure that my legs will hold out that long.

The sensation that everyone is watching me is still strong, but my legs are working better. I know Richard won't be in town, but who knows who might spot me? I stick out in the crowd of elderly shoppers. Head down, I find I can march. I can see the station. The closer I get, the harder it becomes to walk. At the ticket queue, the trembling returns. I made it this far and I'm determined not to falter. I lock my knees and shuffle forward. All I have to do is ask for a ticket.

"Yes, please."

"Um … what time is the next train to London?"

"You've just missed it. There won't be one for another hour. Platform 1."

An hour! A fucking hour! I can't be sitting in public for an hour. The school might ring home. If they do, Richard will find me before then. Shit! What do I do? I could hide in the toilets for an hour. No, that's stupid. I…

"Do you want a ticket?"

"Um. Yes I do. What time's the next train?"

"To where?"

"Just the next train."

"Platform 3 to Crewe. It leaves in five minutes."

"Yeah. A single to Crewe please."

"Will you be returning within three months. It's the same price."

"No." I'm all confused. I've fucked up, but at least I'll be on the train and out of here in five minutes. I pay and take the ticket. I can see the train. I speed up as I cross the bridge, but struggle to walk down the stairs. One slip and I've blown it. Don't go without me please.

Walking along the platform I pass under a clock with no body. I put my head down, so it doesn't see me. I step into the first open carriage, sit down in a seat and huddle myself as small and out of view as is possible. I wait.

'Shut the doors and move will you.'

How many times I think this before the train begins to pull away, I don't know. It's too slow for my liking, but it's picking up speed, getting faster and further away from that horrid hateful place. From the unfamiliar angle, I watch the buildings and the streets that I recognise, pass by until there are no more houses - no more Northampton. Only green, trees, bushes, grass and fields of sheep and cows. The rhythm of the train rocks a little bit of calmness into me. I am away, at last. I don't have a clue where Crewe is and I don't care. No one will expect me to go to a place I've never heard of.

The train slows and stops. My nerves kick back in; I don't want it to stop. To my relief, it's only a matter of seconds before it starts moving again, but I'm still on a high alert. My nerves are shot and I wonder if I'll spend the rest of my life in this state. As the train gets faster and the miles are left behind, my anxiety eases a little.

Another stop, a longer one this time, and I'm back to a trembling wreck. I see a policeman on the platform and my breathing stops. I want to dive under the seat, but I can't move. I bet he's looking for me. No, I'm being silly. Even if Richard knows that I've disappeared the police wouldn't be looking for me this quickly. The train pulls away; the policeman is still on the platform.

As I catch my breath, I find I can think clearer. I go back through my footsteps and realise the stupid mistakes that I've made. A terrifying fear grips me by the throat and pins me to the chair.

The ticket seller might have already called the police.

If I had bought a ticket to London, waited and got on the train like a normal person, I would have gone unnoticed. Nobody goes to a train station and asks what time the next train to 'anywhere' is. Not unless they want to throw themselves under it or they're a runaway. I bet the ticket sellers are used to strange behaviour, and recognising the real passengers from runaways and suicidals. She's probably already alerted the police. She'll have told them that I'm going to Crewe. They'll be waiting for me at the station and they'll take me back home. I have to get off this train before it gets to Crewe. I don't even know if there is another stop before Crewe; I don't know how far Crewe is or where in the country it is. For all of my wanting the train to go faster, only an hour ago, now I want it to stop. I have to get off.

The crowd of soldiers that are sitting at the other end of the carriage are getting louder and rowdier. I think they're drinking. Maybe if I get off at the same stop as them, I can mingle in. They're all in green uniforms; I'll be camouflaged amongst them. I can't risk it though. They might not get off until Crewe. I watch them as the train speeds across the countryside. I need to think and fast before it stops again. If the next platform turns out to be Crewe, I'll get amongst them. If it's some place else, I'll get off and … and.

The train slows. I strain my neck searching for the sign to tell me where I am. The overhead speaker says something, but it's crackly and nasal. It sounds like Richard, but I don't catch a word of what it says, and I never want to hear that voice again.

More tracks appear either side of the train. Rows and rows of houses and buildings are to the left and right of me. The train continues slowly, but there's still no sign of a platform. The buildings get larger and denser. This is a huge town, far bigger than Northampton. I pray it isn't Crewe.

Huge black brick walls appear, either side, blocking my view of the landscape. Slowly the train heaves itself along. I can see a sign in the distance. Don't be Crewe.

As we approach the sign, I can see it has too many letters to be Crewe. Closer and closer -- 'Birmingham, New street'.

What a relief. My stomach is all over the place with butterflies, excitement, fear and nausea. The soldiers are leaving their seats and huddling around the door. The train stops and I follow them out on to the platform, through the ticket man and into a huge shopping centre - I wasn't expecting that. The soldiers go into a pub and I'm left exposed. I have to do something about it and quick; there are police here and I am a criminal.

I walk and try to look like I know where I'm going. The place is packed with people - all kinds of different people - it couldn't be more perfect. The illusion is shattered by a kick in my arse. I turn around and two girls are right behind me.

"Don't you know it's lethal to wear a parka round here?"

I stare in dismay at them. What a nice welcome to my new home. Four black men are close behind them and one intervenes.

"Come on Sue. Leave de girl alone - she's probly not from round here and don't know de rules." He puts his arm around me. "You best get out o' here or dump de jacket, Sweetie."

I pull away from him and walk into a shop. I browse the shelves for a while - hoping they'll all carry on to where they were going. I need to do something - something drastic. I spot Boots the chemist on the other side of the arcade. I check the coast is clear to cross and make my way through the bustle.

I consider stealing some make-up. I don't want to spend my life's savings, but it's too risky. I'll have to buy it - I need a disguise. I'll go for a punk look. I use the make-up testers in the shop to paint my face. I look completely different and a lot older. I buy make-up, a comb, hairspray and scissors. I know they're all normal things to buy, but my paranoia tells me that the shop assistant is suspicious of my intentions - especially when I ask her where the toilets are.

In the toilets, I hack off my neat little black bob. Well, it did make me look like Snow White and so young. The remainder of my hair I spray and spike into tufts. I take off my parka and spread it out on the floor. I undress and fold my extra clothes placing them on my coat. I cut my black school skirt into half its original length. I flush my tie and my blazer badge down the toilet. I put my few belongings on the pile of clothes before tying the strings and hood of my parka together, tucking the sides in to form what looks like a bag. I stand in front of the mirror and admire my creation. In my baggy red jumper, tiny black skirt, monkey boots and with a new head, I'm no longer me anymore. Even my own mother wouldn't recognise me. It is fantastic and beyond what even I imagined possible.

Leaving the toilets, there's a bounce in my step. My legs are strong again. I get some odd looks from passers-by and some little kids whistle at me and hide, but I don't mind being noticed now because I'm a different person; I'm a grown up. I don't even feel the urge to tell them to fuck off - an adult wouldn't do that.

Walking out of the arcade I catch the chill of the air around my legs, but the sun is shining and I'm free.

Move On

Wandering for a while through the unfamiliar streets, I notice the vast mixture of races and classes of people. It's very different from Northampton. I spot a patch of green through the bustle and the buildings. It looks like a park. I head towards it expecting something resembling my own park. It isn't that big at all; it's the smallest park I've ever seen. There are a lot more people about, but they don't seem interested in the surroundings. There are people in suits rushing in every direction. The people on the benches are reading newspapers held high and hiding their faces. A roller-blader wearing headphones whizzes past me. It's nothing like my park.

I sit down on the grass and check my luggage. Most importantly my money; I can't lose that. I don't have a clue how far I've come. It was only a few train stops, but this place could be a world away in a different galaxy. The first place Richard will look for me is London because that's where I was thinking of going, and he seems to have a knack of reading my mind. When he receives the information about Crewe, he'll go looking there. Although today didn't go to plan, and I thought I'd die of heart failure, it has worked out even better than I could have imaged.

I can't spend all day and night in the park. I need to get to know someone, but everyone is so busy. I notice that people bump into each other and don't even stop to say sorry. I'd speak to anyone in my own park, but here I'm an outsider and my appearance is slightly hostile. They might think I'm a mugger or a prostitute, or even a nutter. For a public place, there is no interaction between the people. I need to find some place where there is.

Museum, Art gallery? No, people go to those places as couples or families. Library? No, you can't talk in a library. Pub - I've never been in a pub. I've seen them on telly, and everyone talks to anyone in a pub. I look old enough to go to the pub, I'm confident enough to walk in and ask for a coke and stand at the bar, but I'm going to need a reason for being in the bar alone. I could say I'm waiting for a friend from Uni. It makes me sound older too. I might get asked what I'm studying. Damn, what do I know enough about to be studying at University? Astronomy! I know how far the moon is from the earth; I'll say I'm studying astronomy. I'm frightened that I won't be able to pull it off, but it's only lying - little lies - I can lie.

"Hello."

I look up to see a funny little man wearing thick glasses.

"Hello," I reply.

"You don't mind if I sit here to read do you?"

"No sure."

I pull my bag tight against my thigh. The book in his hand is the Bible. A creepy sensation hones in on me - it's dreamlike. Is he an angel sent to me when I most need help?

"What's your name?" he asks, settling himself beside me, and placing the Bible on his lap.

"Jes," I reply after some hesitation. I nearly said Jesus - well it's the first thing that came into my head.

"I'm David. It's a pleasure to meet you." He holds out his hand and I do the same. He grips my hand tightly; too tightly for his little frame, and for my liking.

I watch the people scuttling about like insects, as David reads his book. I'm waiting for something to happen - for him to speak again. He must be here for a reason. I look across to him, as I try to think of something to rekindle the conversation. I see the book in his hand doesn't contain the tiny words of the Bible that I was expecting, but porno pictures of naked people fucking. I turn away pretending I haven't noticed. I want to stand up and kick him in the head, but I can't risk getting arrested. Jumping to my feet I say, "Anyhow, I have to go." I walk away from him shaking with anger.

"I hope to see you again … soon," he calls after me.

Fuck! I could run back and kick his head in right now. I don't - I keep walking. I now have a name; I'm no longer Marie.

Pub. I have to find a pub. Pubs are usually on corners in residential areas. To find a friendly pub, I'll have to get out of the shopping area. I accept that I'll be turned away from some for not being old enough - they won't all be so strict. I could even ask for a job. I stop at a shop window and check out my reflection. I'm proud of it, but it's hardly going to get me a job anywhere. I breathe in deeply and say to my reflection. "Hello Jes." I'll be rumbled if I don't get used to answering to my new name.

My arse is smacked really hard. I jump against the glass and I nearly piss myself, shit myself and throw up, all at the same time. I want to run - instead I freeze. Only my head turns slightly to see what attacked me.

The group of soldiers from the train are trailed along the street. They make a whooping noise; I assume to the soldier that slapped my arse. I glare at the guy directly behind me then turn to face him.

"Are you seriously thinking of joining the army? Or are you just admiring yourself in the window," he asks with a soft Scottish accent. His arms twitch. He looks younger than the others, and I'm sure he would've said and done nothing had he been alone. His mates slap his back as they pass him. "She'll eat you alive, pretty boy."

I'm unsure how to react until he points up to the sign above the shop. I turn, step back and read it. It's an army recruitment office. We both laugh. I'm ashamed to tell him that I was looking at myself and totally unaware of the shop.

"Where are you lot going dressed like that?"

"We're on our way home - to Scotland. We're staying here tonight before we go our separate ways. Mike knows a guy who's letting us stay at his house. Do you fancy coming for a drink?"

My immediate instinct is to say yes. He can't be more than twenty years old. I was heading for a pub after all, but the experience I'd had in the park makes me more wary. I wonder what strange twist this scenario will create. The choice is taken from me, as he grabs my arm, pulling me along. "I don't want'a lose 'em, Hen."

We catch up with his mates, as they pile into a pub on the corner. I link his arm and blend in with the exotic and eccentric characters in the pub. The soldiers are the oddity, as they're all dressed the same.

"What do you want to drink?"

"Just a coke, thanks."

"Really. You'll need something stronger than that if you're gonna party with us."

"Maybe later. I'll have a coke for now."

I nip out to the toilet for the usual and check my appearance. I'm not used to wearing so much make-up, and I imagine that I've smudged it all over my face. It's perfectly fine. I have to pull myself away from the mirror. I could stare at my transformation for hours. I am a different person. My name is Jes.

Some of the guys are playing pool - others are sitting and standing at the bar. My new friend is sitting at a table with our drinks.

A few cheers and a few groans echo around me, as I join him. "What's all that about?"

"They were taking bets on you climbing out of the toilet window and running away."

"How much did *you* win?"

"Enough. I could tell you weren't the type to run away."

"No. Hot in here isn't it?"

"Nah'ts not. It must be you. What's ya name?"

"Jes."

"Just Jes? Short and sweet. It suits ya. I'm Scott."

"Suits you too, Scott."

A fat guy comes and joins us. He tells us dirty jokes and pokes fun at me. Not in a horrible way; it's quite a good laugh.

I find myself laughing more than I've ever laughed in my life. The cokes keep coming and even the unfunny jokes have me in fits of giggles.

Just as another fat guy comes to join us, one of the soldiers stands at the door. I guess it's Mike. "Come on lads drink up. We need to get closer to home. Follow me."

Everyone downs their drinks and follows him. I stand and stumble into the table. "Careful Jes. Do you want me to carry you?"

"No. I'll be fine. Gimme your arm." I thought that coke tasted funny. I'll be a bit more careful in the next pub.

We go from one pub to another. I haven't

spent any money and nobody seems to care. I tip my drinks into others' glasses when they're not looking. I don't want to get drunk - I've never been drunk before. If I end up in hospital or a police cell, I'll be sent home.

Surprisingly, I don't get refused service in any of the pubs for being too young. It's probably because I'm with the soldiers, but maybe I really do look grown up to everyone. We are refused entry at a couple of pubs, but not due to me. Some of the soldiers are too drunk and one landlord says it's because they're in uniform and it might offend his customers. I might come back to these places tomorrow and ask for a job. I'm quite at home here.

Scott falls gently forward. His face rests on the table. I cling to his arm, making it clear to all that I'm with him while he sleeps. I watch and wonder how the other soldiers can drink so much. They are singing and dancing, raising stools above their heads with one hand and falling off stools in all directions. Every one of them is happy though. This is the most happiness I've ever seen.

"Taxi. Four taxis," a voice bellows over the thundering crowd. The soldiers neck their drinks. I try to wake Scott with a little shake, but he doesn't respond. I pull him up to a sitting position.

"Scott. Wake up. We have to go."

He stirs. His eyes open - the balls rolling in their sockets. I wrap his arm over my shoulder and lift him to his feet. He can't weigh much more than me. He says something that I don't understand.

"Please try to walk. We have to get in the taxi. You can sleep then."

I drag him a little way before I'm aided by a big guy who lifts Scott off his feet, through the door and into the back of the taxi. I climb in beside him. Everyone is too drunk to notice they have a stowaway, or maybe they don't care. Scott slumps against me. He dribbles saliva down my front, as he sleeps off the drink on the journey to Mike's friend's house. The singing continues around me.

Expecting a huge house, I'm shocked when we stop outside a very small house on a council estate. I wonder whether Mike's friend is expecting so many guests. I hope so because it's bloody cold tonight.

Scott wakes up enough to stagger down the path with my support. Inside the guys have spread through the house taking up every bed, couch and chair. Scott and I sit down in a corner by a radiator. He soon wriggles down into a sleeping position on the floor. I join him, putting my bag under my head for a pillow and safekeeping. I link my arm through his and fall asleep to a chorus of snoring coming from every room in the house. I sleep well considering the uncomfortable position on the hard floor.

I wake to jeering shouts and laughs.

"Got yourself a bird for the night and you're still a virgin, Scotty." Sitting up I see all the guys sitting around the room, drinking cups of tea and coffee. I can't believe I've been lying here asleep with all these men in the room and no one tried to fuck me. I don't want them to, but I'm so - well - surprised.

"Scott, you virgin poofta. Or are you a morning guy? Are you gonna show us what you're made of?" the fat soldier says, throwing a cigarette packet at Scott's head.

"Fuck off, you lot." Scott sits up and rubs his eyes.

"You're gonna have to show him how it's done, Lassie."

I sneer at the soldier. I could quite easily get on top of Scott and give them all a show, it wouldn't bother me in the slightest. I'm not me now though. I'm Jes. I don't need to dilute Richard anymore, so they can go fuck themselves.

The fat one still stares at me. There is something about the look on his face that I recognise - an evil look. I've seen it so many times before. I want a piss, but I'm afraid the soldier will follow me to the toilets.

"Scott, I'm going to make a coffee. Do you want one?" I kiss his forehead and pick up my bag.

"Yeah - I'd love one - what's the time?"

Why does he care what the time is? I take my watch off and hand it to him. "Press the bottom button. It'll remind you of home."

Scotland the brave squeaks out, as I go through to the kitchen. I walk straight out of the back door, through the little garden into a car park.

I have a piss between two cars and head for a main road.

Scott is a nice lad, but they're all heading home for Scotland today via different modes of transport, and he doesn't know me well enough to be taking me home to his parents. He might even be married for all I know. One thing I do know is that fat bastard would have raped me if he'd got half the chance. Well fuck that for a game of soldiers.

Unwashed and Somewhat Slightly Dazed

My face must be a mess. Who cares? No one knows me. Trying to find a main road is a nightmare. I seem to be going round in circles and hitting dead ends. Over half an hour I've wandered around this rat run of an estate before I spot a bus stop. I figure all the buses must go to the town centre eventually, so I stand and wait. Shuddering at the thought of what the fat soldier might have done, I wish I'd said something to the others. He might stay over at one of their houses one night. He might rape their sisters or their mothers. They probably would have laughed at me. Nobody thinks that kind of stuff really happens and especially by people known to them. Why I feel the need to save the world is a mystery. I should be thinking about me. Where am I going to go now?

A bus comes into view; its sign reads City Centre. I hope it's got heating.

Stepping onto the bus I'm confronted by a Perspex shield window. Searching for a slot to pay the driver raises my anxiety. It's only a bus - how difficult can it be? I wave a five pound note at the window. The driver doesn't even look at me. He points up to my right where a ticket machine is fixed to the panel. Reading the instructions it says, 'Correct money only - No change given'. I don't know how much the fare is, but I do know the passengers are getting pissed off. They tut and fold their arms. All eyes are on me again - so much for being inconspicuous.

The fiver goes into the machine and a ticket pops out. The bus starts moving before I've sat down and I bump a few passengers on my way to a seat. I look for two free seats. I've noticed I seem to attract nutters; I'm avoiding encouraging another situation.

My mind wanders back home. I wonder what is happening in the house. It's been twenty-four hours since I went missing. The police will be involved by now. It's not only Richard I'm scared of, but the police. They'll be so mad at me for running away and wasting their time, they might arrest me. Then I'll have a criminal record. I'll never get a job or have a future. The urgency to get back to the city centre, and get myself made up again, makes the journey take forever.

The bus stops by some shops that I recognise from yesterday. Getting off I say thank you to the driver. He doesn't reply, and I don't hear any of the other people say thank you. They must think I'm an alien - an awkward alien.

I head to the shopping centre, back to the toilets and wash my face before plastering it in pale make-up and black eyeliner. My hair is lob-sided due to the way I slept. What a state I am. I wet it, spray it and spike it up into tufts. Now I look like I'm a state on purpose, not like a homeless tramp.

The plan to settle here and get a job has been dismissed. All the pubs are closed this time of day, and I'll only draw attention to myself if I wander around the shops all morning. I don't like being so close to the station either. If I've been rumbled for the journey to Crewe then all stations between might be being checked. I'm going to choose a direction and keep walking. I'll leave it to fate as to where I end up.

I walk for miles, for hours. Street after street of houses, high rise flats, industrial estates and graffiti make me think this town ... city never ends. I keep my eye on the sun, so I know I'm not going around in circles. The dismay of not getting anywhere slows my pace and my enthusiasm until I cross a bridge and see a river below it and a wide open green space - a park. Dark clouds hide the sun, but it doesn't matter now - the green has lifted my spirits. I can follow the river - they never go round in circles.

Steps lead down to the river and a path runs alongside. It starts to rain, so I put my parka bag under my jumper. It doesn't make sense to get everything wet. Hopefully I can find a place to dry off and change later. As I walk through the park a few boats pass me and reaching the end of the park I see a lock. I realise it's not a river at all, but a canal. This is better still, as canals are dead straight, so I'll get somewhere quicker and the towpath will never run out. I have a spring in my step and my mind is focused on somewhere nice.

Without resting once, I walk and walk. Boats, people, dogs and ducks pass by me, but there is nothing promising in sight. The water to my right, and the trees and shrubs to my left can be seen way ahead of me - step after step. After hours of walking, hunger pangs twist my stomach - I really should have bought some food in town. I am soaked through with rain and it's getting heavier. The soles of my feet are stinging like burns, but I can withstand the pain. I might not be able to walk at all tomorrow though.

Mile after mile of nothingness, I need to rest, but I'm frightened that if I stop I'll never get up again. Ten more steps then another ten. I force myself to go on and spot what looks like brickwork in the distance. It could be a house or a pub - come on - ten more - ten more.

Reaching the brickwork I find it is a building, but not what I was hoping for. It's the size of a double garage with an open front. Old, rusty chains hang from the back walls, and the ground is ankle deep with rubbish and dead leaves. It's a shelter of some kind - probably for horses in the past. It'll shelter me from the rain and I can change into some dry clothes. Kicking the debris to one side, I make a space to undress. I hang the wet clothes on the chains, and I put on everything else I've got. I wrap my parka tightly around myself and huddle for warmth in the corner of the building. I wait for the rain to stop.

The rain doesn't stop. Darkness falls and it falls fast - pitch darkness and silence. I close my eyes; I should try to sleep. It must only be five or six in the afternoon, but I've never known how dark darkness really is. It's terrifying - it's like being dead. I'm tired enough to sleep, but not warm enough. The cold keeps me from drifting off and then the silence is broken. Strange, noisy creatures scuttle around outside. Grunts, screeches, howls and hoots echo against the walls of the shelter. I know there are no wolves in England. There are no such things as monsters, vampires or other evils from films and books. There is nothing that can harm me. Wild animals are more scared of humans than the other way around. They'll smell me and avoid me. I sit, eyes closed tight, in the corner telling myself these things over and over.

Newspaper images take over my thoughts. 'Panthers and lions loose on the moors. Fields of sheep found ripped apart. Twenty foot python found in a garden pond.' I have never been so terrified in my life. I thought Richard was scary, but he's predictably scary. This is something different. I'm blind and I don't know what creature might attack me or when. I thought the night before my escape was the longest night of my life; it is being surpassed now.

Awake, alert, and petrified, I wait for the sun to rise.

Fantastic Voyage

As the sun rises, my sight is restored; the real world is still here. Birdsong fills the air and I sleep. I sleep half the day away.

When I wake, I'm unsure of which parts of last night were real and which I might have dreamt. All I know is that it was terrifying and I'm not spending another night like it. I wonder how tramps and homeless people manage to get any sleep. It's probably why they take drugs and drink so much.

As I rise from the corner, my joints ache with pain. I straighten my back an inch at a time, and stretch my arms into the air. This must be how it feels to be old. Each step I take, towards my wet clothes, sends a shooting fire from my soles into my feet and ankles. I fear my boots are full of blood and blistered skin. It wouldn't be a good idea to take them off and look; I might not be able to get them on again. I have to get on my way and find somewhere to stay. At least I'm dry, the rain has stopped and the sky is clear of storm clouds.

I take down the clothes from the chains; they're still wet. I wrap them in my soggy jumper, and I leave the shelter to the beasts of the night. With painful footsteps, each making me wince, I hobble along the monotonous towpath once more. After a hundred or so yards, the pain eases, and the winter sunshine warms my skin, penetrating through into my cold, damp bones.

Boats pass by going in the same direction as me. There must be something ahead; they must be going somewhere. Surely they have to refuel or stop to buy food.

I spot something in the distance on the other side of the canal. My worries leave my mind; it's a fisherman. Oh, wouldn't it be great if it was Dave. He could take me somewhere warm in his car. I'm not stupid though - of course it won't be Dave, but I could stop for a chat. I know a little about fishing, and I might find out how far this canal continues before reaching civilisation. I quicken my step looking into the water. I wonder how the fish get in the canal if the sections are blocked by locks. I suppose they could pass through them with the boats. The green, still water sprinkled with patches of brown foam doesn't look like anything could live in it.

I reach a point opposite the fisherman. He looks old. A hat is pulled down over his eyes; I guess he's sleeping. I'm embarrassed to call over to him, but I long to find out if I'm close to getting off this track I can't bear to spend another night in the open.

"Excuse me."

He raises his hand, pushes his hat up and focuses on me. His head jerks once showing me I have his attention.

"Do you know where the next village or town is please?"

He points in the direction I'm going. "That way."

"Do you know how far?"

"Walking distance. Just keep walking that way."

"Thanks." Well that was fucking helpful. I'm sure he was taking the piss and not dumb. At least I know there's something - soon I hope. I continue to walk - on and on - and then I see a bridge. My mind rushes ahead of me - if it's a bridge, there's a road. If there's a road, there'll be traffic, and signs, and people, and houses. Everything's going to be fine. I'll be able to get off this canal and find a bed to sleep in tonight. My plan was to make my money last as long as possible, but I'd hand it all over to sleep in a warm, safe bed tonight.

I walk up the bank by the old, stone bridge. It's a road bridge all right - a very narrow road bridge. It looks like the track once had a covering of tarmac on it, but only thin patches at the edges remain. To the left it disappears into the distance; to the right it bends out of view. There are no road signs. I don't know which way to go. I don't have a clue where in the country I am. I'm thirsty, hungry and tired of walking. I bounce myself up onto the wall of the bridge and dangle my legs over the edge. As I stare down into the still, green water, I count how many times I've wanted to cry in the last three days. The silence is broken by the sound of an engine in the distance. Looking up I see a boat coming towards me. I stare back into the water.

The chugging of the engine gets louder mixed with the sound of laughter and voices. It makes me want to cry even more, but I don't.

"Afternoon," a voice calls out. The boat passes below me. An odd-looking man is looking up at me; he passes under the bridge. A girl is steering at the back of the boat, and as she passes below me she waves, smiles and says, "Hello." I ignore the fucking happy people.

Their boat sends fumes up into my face as it splutters below me. I turn away from the stench and jump down onto the road. I have a choice to make - left or right along the road. Not a single car has driven either way so far; the road might not even be in use anymore. I cross it and look over the other side of the bridge watching the little boat chug into the distance. What was I thinking? They seemed like the friendliest of people, and I completely ignored their welcome. Just because they're moving in a boat doesn't mean they're unapproachable. It's not like a train that can't stop. I could have asked them for a lift. I could kick myself.

Maybe it's not too late. If I run, I can catch up with them. I slip down the bank back onto the towpath. I jog and walk, jog and walk. It's hard because I'm hungry and thirsty. Although my legs are strong they aren't built for running. They press down hard into the ground and give me the spring, but they don't propel me forward. How I wish I had my bike right now.

I stop for breath and realise I haven't gained any ground on them. 'God, will something just go right for once?' I'm unsure if I thought that or said it out loud, but within seconds I see seven people jump off the boat and onto the towpath. I start jogging again. They're approaching a lock, and the boat is coming to a stop. I have plenty of time to catch up.

As I approach, I walk calmly to gather my breath. They look quite young; I'd say in their twenties. They get the lock open and the man that had greeted me earlier drives the boat in. I can't figure out how old he is. I reach them as they're closing the lock gate.

"Can I help?" I ask the girl that had waved to me.

"Sure. Just push."

We push the lock gate closed. People are running all over the place. The boat sinks lower as the water drops. We stand and watch.

"I'm Jes," I say to the girl.

"Thanks Jes. I'm Debbie. What are doing out here? You don't look like a jogger."

"Er…no. I'm kind of lost. You couldn't give me a lift to the nearest town could ya?"

"I can't see why not. I'll introduce you to Richard when we've got through the lock. He's the organiser - Captain he likes to be called. Come on."

Great another fucking Richard. I help push open the other lock gate, Richard drives through and pulls the boat in close to the bank. Everyone gets back on board. I follow Debbie.

Richard jumps off the back of the boat and walks down the towpath to join us at the front.

"And who have we here? Have you found a new friend, Debbie?"

"Yes. This is Jes, and she needs a lift if that's okay."

"Welcome Jes. You can call me Captain." He holds out his hand and I shake it.

"Thank you."

"Where are you heading?" he asks, still holding my hand.

"The next town or village. I'm kind of lost. I was walking my dog and he vanished. I went looking for him, but ended up lost myself." I wonder why I'm making up this stupid story. I don't have to answer to him. I still can't figure his age. He looks old because his hair is white, his eyebrows are white, and the pupils of his eyes are colourless and pale like old people's eyes, yet his skin and his body are that of a twenty year old.

"How long have you been lost for?"

"I don't know. All day."

"Is there some place in particular you want to go? We're not in any rush."

"No. Anywhere's fine. I can find my way home once I'm on a road."

"So where's home? It can't be far from here."

"I don't … You wouldn't have heard of it. It's a tiny village."

He lets go of my hand. I know he knows I'm lying.

"Debbie take Jes inside and get her something to eat and drink. Whose turn is it to steer?"

Debbie leads me inside as Richard organises setting off. She makes me a tuna sandwich and offers me a can of coke, but I want water. We sit down at a small table. I'm not a fan of tuna, but it tastes like the best thing I've ever eaten. I drink the water down in one.

"Could I have another glass please - I'm so thirsty."

"Of course. You can have anything you like. We share everything here. You seem a little reluctant to answer questions Jes. It's okay though. You can tell me anything, or ask me anything and I'll share it with you."

"Is Captain an albino?"

"Haha. No he's not. I know he looks like he is, but he didn't always look that way. When Richard, oops, Captain was ten years old he was struck by lightning. It turned every hair on his body white. He died in the hospital and went to heaven. He spoke with God about his untimely death and blamed Him for it. God gave him another chance on the condition that he devotes his life to God and his children. Can you image it?"

"No. That's very ... weird."

"Hmm, and God works in mysterious ways. I'm sure R ... Captain will be down soon to have a chat with you once we're up to speed again."

She is right. He walks down the steps into the kitchenette and Debbie rises and walks through a curtain into another part of the boat. Captain sits down next to me and places my hand between both of his.

"Are you feeling any better after some sustenance?"

"Yes thank you. I was getting thirsty."

"Dear, dear Jes. You can't keep things from me. I know you are lost. You've been lost for a long time. That is why God has brought us all here - together at this spot - for your salvation. I knew this boat trip idea had a greater meaning when I dreamt of a lost lamb the night before we embarked on this journey. You are that lamb, Jes. You can tell me your real name if you like."

I have to give him credit for being a twisted, manipulating freak, and he may have fooled all his little disciples, but I'm used to this kind of shit. It's all a bluff. If he's as 'all seeing', as he's making out then he'd know what my name is.

"My name is Jes."

"So be it Jes. I have a story I want you to read. I'll find it for you, and you can read at your leisure."

A girl passes through the boat, as he gets up to leave.

"Sue, meet Jes. She's going to be staying with us for a while."

"Welcome Jes." She bows her head.

"Hi."

Captain goes through the curtain and Sue turns as she walks up the steps to the deck. The welcoming face she'd just greeted me with has definitely transformed into a sneer.

I'm left alone for a few minutes to ponder whether there are actually any normal people in the world.

The captain appears through the curtain with a book in his hand. "Come Jes. You must rest."

I follow him back through the boat. He points out where the toilet is and pulls back a curtain revealing a small room the size of a very narrow single bed. He pulls down a panel, clicks things into place and drags out a thin mattress and blanket from a slot above his head.

"That's clever."

"Isn't it? There's as much room in this boat as a six bed-roomed house if you utilise the space efficiently. I'll get you a cushion. Here." He hands me the book. 'St. Anthony of Lost Things.'

He returns with a cushion and puts his hand on my cheek. "Now rest my child. Read and rest. We'll talk again later."

I nod, as he pulls the curtain across and leaves me alone. I sit on the bed, open the book and hold it against my chest in case he comes back. There's a small round window that I can watch through for any sign of houses or life. We pass nothing but trees and sky for hours.

The smell of hot food wafts past my nose.

Stronger and stronger the aroma fills the boat. It's not that it's the greatest smelling of meals, but it's the first sniff I've had of hot food in days.

As darkness falls, the boat slows and bumps against the wall of the canal. I guess this is as far as we're going today.

Debbie's head pops around the curtain. "Hey. Dinner time."

I follow her through to the front of the boat. The little kitchenette, that I'd sat in earlier, has quadrupled in size and a table is set for nine. I sit down next to Debbie. Everyone is silent. There are three young men and two other girls at the table, their heads down. I put my head down too. Richard, Sue and another girl are dishing up the food and serving it round the table. Sausages, mash and cabbage. It smells a lot nicer than it looks, but I'm not complaining - it's free.

When everyone is seated Richard says a prayer. Some of the others join in - some mouth the words only speaking 'Amen'. I manage a slightly delayed 'Amen' before tucking into the food.

I have so many questions I want to ask them, but we eat in silence. It gives me time to think, and maybe it's a good idea to say nothing at this point. I have no intention of staying with these people, but a good night's sleep and some breakfast can't do any harm.

After the meal Debbie starts to collect the plates. "Do you need a hand?" I ask.

Captain replies for her, "Thank you, Jes. You

and Debbie can do the washing up this evening. That was kind of you to offer. I know you're going to get on well here with us."

The table is folded away and disappears somewhere. A guitar strums along to the singing voices behind me, as I wash the dishes in the smallest sink I've ever seen. Debbie dries them, as I pass them to her. She is singing along too. I jiggle my head, so it looks like I'm enjoying myself.

Just as I'm thinking it's not so bad, an elbow thumps me in the back. "Sorry. I slipped. This boat just isn't big enough for so many of us." It's Sue and she's smiling. I know she did it on purpose. I give her back the same evil look that she'd given me earlier, and continue with the dishes.

Captain reads a rota out for the morning chores, but he doesn't mention my name. He notices me looking.

"I'll have a chat with you before 'lights out', Jes."

'Lights out'. What is this - some kind of prison ship?

Everyone leaves to go to their own spaces or beds, except Captain. "Sit down, Jes."

I do, though I don't like being alone with him.

"Now Jes. I'd like you to stay with us on our little holiday. It will bring peace to your soul. Would you consider it?"

The only peace I need is for the soles of my feet. If I can travel by boat instead of walking, and put up with their singing and their crazy notions that Captain has conversations with God, then my answer has to be yes.

"Yes. I would like to stay for a while longer. I'd like to help out too. What do you want me to do tomorrow?"

"All the jobs are taken for tomorrow, but you can help one of the others. I'll let you decide in the morning, and you'll be able to get to know some of them. I'm glad you've decided to stay - that's what God wanted too. Do you have any possessions with you?"

"Only some damp clothes, make-up and a comb."

"Well, we share everything here. So don't get upset if someone wants to borrow them. It works both ways. If you need anything, just ask. You can go now. Sleep well."

I walk back to my bed. It's lucky I didn't mention the money - he'll have me sharing that out. I stuff it into my bra in case anyone goes through my belongings.

He said Sue and another girl had to go for supplies tomorrow; I wonder if that means we'll be near a town. At least she'll be off the boat and not bothering me. She's got something against me. I don't know why, but I can tell she's not a nice person. I won't dwell on it; it's nice to be warm and comfy. I'm sure I'll sleep well tonight.

It doesn't turn out to be as good a night's sleep as I was expecting. The boat creaks to start with. I'm sure there are people walking around. It rocks and grinds to giggles and whispers that sound so close. Someone is having sex. I can hear every groan. A loud cry of "I'm coming!" confirms it's Captain. Well, if this is his idea of sharing everything, he can fuck his boat up his fucking arse. And if he comes anywhere near me, I'll kill him.

The noise quietens and the rocking stops. I want to leave now, but I'm afraid of what's out there. I will leave in the morning. I sleep lightly.

The Width of a Circle

"All hands on deck in ten minutes!"

Shit. I just want to sleep; I could sleep all day long if I had some peace. The boat rocks as everyone scurries about on Captain's orders.

After what I heard last night, I've changed my plan. I'm going to go with Sue to do the shopping and give them the slip. I can't stay here another night.

I have a wash once the sink is free. There is a shower, but I'm not taking my clothes off like the others do. They walk around half naked. One of the guys is naked apart from a towel on his head. I catch his reflection in the mirror, as I put on my make-up; my whole body shudders and my undercarriage muscles tighten up.

My image complete, I make my way up to the small deck where everyone is huddled together.

"Right, let's get everything shipshape and we'll head off. We should reach dry land in about two and half hours." What a dick he is.

Those that have jobs to do scuttle off and get the boat started. I follow Debbie as she collects the dirty clothes that need washing. "Do you want a change of clothes, Jes? I'm taking the washing to the laundrette. There are plenty of spare clothes in that cupboard."

"No, I'm fine, but you can take these." I hand her my damp clothes from the day before. I want it to look like I'm sticking around. I know I could jump off the boat and run away, but a deep rooted fear tells me that they'll chase me, catch me and imprison me on this boat forever. I know what Richards are like. Soon we'll be at a town. I just hope there are normal people living there.

Captain is cooking the breakfast. It smells like sausages again. "Jes, come and give me a hand in here," he calls. I hate those words, but I go through to the kitchen area trying to look eager to help.

"Would you lay the table?"

"Sorry?"

"Would you mind laying the table. Just for five. The others will have second sitting; they're busy."

I'm sure the first time he said, 'Would you lay on the table.' I must be hearing things again. I set out the cutlery in silence until Captain breaks it.

"Can you drive, Jes?"

"No...I've not had any lessons yet."

"Are you old enough to drive?"

"Yes. I'm eighteen."

"Old enough then."

"I thought I might help Sue and - is it Karen - the other girl who's going shopping? I was thinking of going with Debbie to the laundrette. I've given her some of my clothes, but I thought it would be good to get to know some of the other girls."

"That's a very good idea. Sue can fill you in on a few things. She's a very good girl. Another pair of hands would be very welcome."

I'm not sure if it's me. Everyone seems to

love and admire this man, but everything he says to me has 'creepy innuendo' written all over it. At least my stay on the ark will be brief. Captain won't get the chance to brainwash me into his little cult. I didn't escape from the hell house to spend the rest of my days in a hell boat.

We sit down for breakfast, say our prayers and eat in silence. I swear Sue has kicked my feet at least five times. It might not have been her and it could be accidental, but I'm sure she hates me.

"Sue, Jes will be going with you and Karen to the shops today. You can get to know each other and stretch those legs."

She nods in pleasant agreement then gives me an evil eye, as we finish eating.

I wash the dishes while Richard finishes cooking the second round of breakfast. Debbie takes over the steering and the others tuck into their food. It's all very organised and I daren't speak while they eat. I'm learning, or am I being conditioned? This is like home. I expect one of them to ask Captain, 'Please may I get down?' I can't understand why these people are letting this happen to them. They have a choice; they are grown ups.

After I've cleaned the next round of plates, I go back to my space and pretend to read for a while. After a couple of hours, I spot buildings from the little window and a flurry of excitement and adrenalin energizes my system. The chugging slows and the boat vibrates. A couple of bumps and the engine cuts out. I make my way to the deck and join Sue and Karen. Debbie jumps off with the huge bag of washing. She's always smiling. Even carrying the heavy bag, she walks with a bounce, her pony tail swinging from side to side.

Captain gives Sue a list and some money. "Take your time, we'll be here for at least two hours while Debbie's at the laundrette. And use your initiative - I know you're good at it."

Sue's body language displays the strange chemistry between the two of them. It makes me want to puke, but not literally.

"I'll hunt down the bargains and with the extra pair of hands we'll bring home plenty of goodies," Sue replies, her head tilted up towards his face. I half expect her to kiss him, but she doesn't.

The three of us hop off the boat and walk through the little village. We pass gift shops, a tea shop, a tourist shop, a little museum and there are an enormous amount of flowers for this time of year. It reminds me of a place we'd go to on school trips when I was at primary school.

I stop dead and turn around. The place is set out exactly the same as I remember it. From this angle I can see it is the same place - it has to be.

"What's the matter?" Sue asks.

"Nothing. I thought I recognised the place that's all. Do you know where we are?"

"You're one thick bitch. You don't know where you are. You don't know where you came from. You ... Oh forget it come on." Her pleasant tone has changed dramatically on dry land.

"Seriously, I don't know where I am."

"You're on the Grand Union canal." Well that wasn't helpful. I decide to stay quiet for a little while. The more I see around me, the more I'm sure this is the same place. If it is, then I'm not far from home. My suspicions are confirmed at a road crossing. The sign reads 'Northampton 6m.' An imaginary spotlight shines down on me. I am vulnerable to attack from the people and the drivers that might recognise me. I quicken my step and squeeze between the two girls shielding myself from the eyes.

"There's no rush, twat."

"I just wanted to ask you some stuff. Do you live on the boat all the time?" I choose not to get riled by her insults.

"You really are a stupid bitch. Of course we don't live on the boat. Every three months we have time together for a week."

"Whose boat is it?"

"It belongs to all of us, including you now."

"So where do you live the rest of the time?"

"In our 'own' places."

Karen is more helpful. "We've all lived with Richard at some point. He's helped us get our lives on track. Some of us were homeless or had drug problems. You wouldn't think it now, looking at us. Sue moved into a new place a couple of weeks ago. None of us would have made anything of our lives if it wasn't for Richard."

I guess Sue is quite new to it all, and that's why she hasn't learnt to be the politest of girls.

"I was quite happy living with Richard. Missy here will be keeping him company now," Sue replied, before turning to me. "How good are you at stealing? I bet you could fit loads of stuff in that coat."

I wasn't expecting that. I look to Karen. "Is she serious?"

Karen smiles. "The Co-op's just up here past the church. Get as much as you can; they won't suspect a thing. We split up and meet back at the boat. It's a piece of cake." Karen is far more pleasant than Sue, but still, they are serious. I'm shocked and I know if anyone gets caught, it'll be me. I lag back a bit. I'm not going in that shop.

"You like Richard don't you?" Sue asks without turning her head.

"He seems okay."

"I think you like him a lot."

"I don't know him well enough."

"What do you think?" Sue asks Karen.

As they slip into conversation with each other, I dart behind a tree, over the wall of the churchyard and scurry through the perimeter bushes to the farthest point behind the church. Knowing I'm out of their sight, I run through the gravestones to a doorway in the church. Turning the handle, the door opens to my disbelief. I tiptoe in and close it silently behind me. Stooping with my bottom on my heels, I creep along the passage into a hall filled with rows of pews. There's no sight or sound of people, but I keep down, and shuffle along a row of benches crawling underneath at the end. They'll never look for me here, and they'll be leaving in two hours. I wish I hadn't dumped my watch.

Being free from Richard hasn't turned out how I was expecting it to at all. I started out running and hiding from him. All I've done in the last few days is continue to run and hide from everyone I've met and it's exhausting. The images of a bustling London, being hidden amongst the crowds, meeting up with similar people and starting a new life were a complete fantasy. I'm lucky that I didn't catch that train to London. I'm sure there would be even worse people there that would have preyed on my naivety. What kind of life would that have been? A short one. Yet here I am hiding under a pew in an empty church from a few God-fearing kids. I don't know where I'm going to sleep tonight or what weirdoes I'll encounter tomorrow. I want to be somewhere safe. I want to go to my park. I should go to my park and kill myself. I've had enough of my life; it will always be like this otherwise. I'll wait until I know the boat will definitely be gone. I'll walk back to Northampton, to the park. There I will find a way to kill myself. If I'm going to die, that's where I want to be. Now … how to die…?

A creaking halts my thoughts and stops my

breath. A door crashes shut. Footsteps echo around the church making it difficult to know how close by they are. Keys jangle and a door slams closed. A key rattles in the lock and the bolt clunks. I hope that wasn't the door that I'd let myself in through.

Waiting a while to be sure that the person has left the building, I go back to my thoughts of how I can die. I don't want it to hurt. Drowning frightens me. I try to imagine what it would be like breathing water instead of air. It sounds simple to put my head in the lake and breathe in water. I've never heard of anyone that's committed suicide by drowning themselves in that way though. It must be harder than I imagine.

Killing myself is a worthy option, but the words 'committing suicide' make we want to fight back. They are words for the weak or the cowardly. I don't want to commit suicide - that'll mean Richard has won - I want to kill myself and that's different.

The thoughts of ropes, suffocation and jumping from a tall tree soon leave my mind, as my belly rumbles with hunger. I must have been here hours. The boat will surely be gone by now. I crawl out of my hiding place and pop my head above the pews. There's nobody about and the sun is shining low in the sky lighting up the paintings on the wall with the vibrant colours from the stained glass.

Wandering from door to door, I'm dismayed that they're all locked. I walk up and down the aisle and try to imagine my wedding day, my husband and who would be sitting in the pews. No visions appear. It's cold here and it's empty, except for me. I'm alone and it will always be like this. Unless I die.

Realising that I could be here for some time, I make a mattress from the kneeling cushions between the pews. The sun drops lower and darkness falls again - pitch darkness. I should have made my escape in the summertime when it's warm and light, but I know I couldn't have waited that long. I daren't put the lights on in case someone spots them. Curled up on the makeshift bed, and using my parka as a blanket, I think about dying from thirst or starvation before falling asleep.

All the Madmen

Awoken by the jangling of keys, I roll under a pew and drag some of the cushions out of view. Someone enters the church. I hold my breath - afraid it will echo around the walls and I'll be discovered. Shuffling footsteps are accompanied by the singing voice of an old lady. The clattering of a metal bucket and broom handles thunders around the church. I'm sure I hear the door open again, but it's hard to distinguish a particular sound as they all bounce off each other.

"Good morning, Phillis." It's a man's voice.

"Good morning, Vicar. And what a beautiful

morning it is." She continues to sing. A floral, disinfectant smell fills the air. She is most likely to be a cleaner, but you can't tell with old people - the smell could be her.

"Indeed. You'd think it was a summer's day if it wasn't for the chill." His voice trails off into the distance. Only the singing voice and the bucket scraping along the stone floor can be heard, and they are getting closer.

A mop pokes me in the leg.

"Jesus, them kids. No respect." She bends down to pick up the cushions and comes face to face with me.

"Oh … Hello, I hope you're not expecting breakfast?"

"I'm sorry. I got locked in." I smile and crawl out from under my parka. She seems friendly enough.

"You're not from round here are you? I know every kid in this village and I've never seen you before. You don't look like a tourist either, or one that would come in here to visit the Lord. Kids like you don't come to church unless you're dragged."

"I came to see the paintings. I'm an art student. I fell asleep, and when I woke up the doors were locked."

"Then you'd know they're not paintings - they're muriels. They're what hold this church up and support the roof."

I hold in my laughter. It's hard to tell if she's deadly serious or having a joke with me. She must have a friend called Muriel.

"Who are you talking to?" the vicar's voice echoes from somewhere out the back. I sit down low in the pew afraid that he'll call the police.

"Who am I speaking to? WHO am I speaking to? Why I'm speaking to God, and I'm speaking to Jesus, and I'm speaking to the God damn devil who lets little children come into the church with chewing gum to stick to the bottoms of the pews. Who do you think I'm bloody well speaking to?" She winks at me and carries on mopping the floor, nodding her head and muttering to herself.

"Well maybe they've heard you this time. I'll be back later. I have an appointment with Mrs. Sinclair." The door closes.

"I bet you do. Mrs. Sin more like," she mutters, as she shoves the mop between the next set of pews.

Rising to my feet, I admire the paintings. They aren't so vibrant in normal light. They do stretch from the floor to the ceiling, and must have looked fantastic in their day. Now they are dull and cracked, and whole chunks of plaster are missing here and there.

"So, won't someone be missing you?" she asks.

I want to speak to her, but I don't know where to start. I need to politely leave and get on my way to the park, but I'm drawn to a part of the mural. Almost hidden by the sloshing of the mop in the bucket, I think I hear her mutter 'ignoramus'. I ignore her and place my hand on the mural over a little lamb - it seems quite poignant after what Captain had said to me. There's a hole in the plaster where its eye should be. Putting my finger in the hole and swirling it around, little crumbs of sandy plaster fall to the floor. Over the years, I imagine kids have sat at this pew, bored by the Sunday service and have scratched and poked at the eye, tunnelling into the lamb's brain. I wonder, why the lamb and why its eye? It's an enormous painting with many things that could have been attacked, yet they chose the little lamb's eye. Scratch after scratch, and poke after poke the damage had got deeper over time, and how many fingers would it have taken to blind the lamb.

"What are you doing, child?" the old woman shouts at me.

Facing her with my finger in the hole where the lamb's eye should be I go to speak, but she's marching towards me with a broom in her hand.

"What do you want being in here?"

"I want to be grown up that's all. I want to be old like you." It just comes out of my mouth; it wasn't meant to sound rude. I was afraid that she was going to attack me with the broom.

"You cheeky little bastard. Go on, get out of here you cheeky little bastard. Fancy speaking to me like that. Go on, go, get out. Cheeky little fucker."

I've already jumped the pew avoiding the lunges of the broom. I run to the door. "Fuck you,

you mad cow." I don't even shut the door. I run and I cry for the first time, but I don't know why. Why now? Maybe because I left my parka under the pew.

Finding my way back to the road sign, I stop and stare at it for a while. I no longer care if anyone sees me. If I'm picked up by the police and taken home, it won't be for long. I'll go to the park instead of school and I'll kill myself. Hopefully it won't come to that. It's only six miles and if I'm not caught, I'll be dead in a few hours.

I walk and think for a while. What happened to David Bowie? He hasn't spoken to me since I left. Maybe he can't find me, or maybe I'm too far away for him to tune in to my head. I should have brought a record with me - he'd have found me then. The loneliness is getting me down; I stop thinking about him.

On the desolate road surrounded by fields, a car slows down beside me. I ignore it. Its horn beeps, but I'm not flinching. It could be the police, it could be Richard or it could be a murderer for all I care. The car drives ahead of me and pulls over in my path. It's a taxi. As I walk around the car past the driver's open window, he asks, "Do you need a ride?"

I don't speak. I pull out my pocket lining indicating that I have no money and continue to walk.

"Don't worry about the money. I'm going this way anyway. There's nothing ahead for miles until you reach Northampton." His car is driving alongside again.

What harm can it do? It'll get me to the park quicker, so I open the passenger door. The car stops and the fat, sweaty taxi driver pats the passenger seat. I get in, but I don't want to talk to him, so I'll pretend I'm foreign.

"Where are you heading?"

I hold out my hands and pull a confused face.

"Where - are - you - going?" Where - are - you - from? Okay. You - tell - me - when - to - stop."

As he drives, he lists nationalities searching my face for recognition while slapping my thigh with his left hand at each guess. I concentrate on memorising his name and number that are printed on the badge dangling from the dashboard. I'm not sure why because if he's a murderer, it's pointless. Anything else he does wouldn't be believed anyway and who would I report him to? I have no intention of going to the police. The taxi driver is running out of nationalities, so the slapping eases. He keeps one eye on the road and the other on my legs. I wish I had my parka.

His knowledge of countries comes to an end, so not wanting him to think I'm an alien, I pat both my ears and murmur in a deep, slow voice, "I'm deaf."

He looks embarrassed then shouts, "I'm sorry - I didn't realise."

It's funny how that has made me less attractive to him. He stops looking at my legs and drives on in silence. We reach a junction with a road sign to Northampton. I point to it and smile. He nods with understanding, as we drive into the built-up area. Approaching a roundabout he holds up his hands and sticks out his bottom lip. I point straight ahead. I wish I'd thought of this before today. I might have had an easier time of things.

Getting closer to the hell house, I slink down in the seat holding my hand up to the side of my face. We stop at some traffic lights and the panic of being trapped in the car, so close to home, overwhelms me.

Pulling open the car door, I leap out. "Cheers for that you filthy fucking letch," I say in a normal voice, slamming the door and running to the nearest alley. I can make it all the way to the park through the alleys. I don't run for long; a fast walk is just as quick and not so tiring.

I see the park across the road. Any one of the cars could be someone looking for me. To think that I have come this far, made a definite decision and am minutes away from ending it all, makes the road itself some kind of trap. There are no bridges, no underpasses, no other way to reach my final destination. I wait peeping from the alleyway for a clear gap in the traffic. My heart thuds and the trembling feeling is returning to my legs. What the hell - I decide to go for it. If my legs don't get me across then I'll get run over. It'll solve my next problem.

I'm in the park. I don't remember running across the road. I must have closed my eyes.

Walking down to the lake, I stay close to the trees and bushes in case I spot someone that I need to hide from. At the top of a slope I can see the whole lake. Nobody is fishing, but a woman and two small children are feeding the ducks. I'll have to wait until they've gone, as it wouldn't be a nice memory for the children to come across a dead body in the park at such a young age.

I head to the spinney with a new idea. Maybe the dope heads can sell me some drugs. I could take an overdose and know nothing of my death. Searching through the bushes where they normally hide, I find nothing but crisp packets, chocolate wrappers and discarded knickers. I wonder if knicker-elastic is strong enough to hang myself with, but realise it's a disgusting idea. Imagine the reputation I'd get.

Finding that the tree log hasn't also abandoned the park, I climb up onto it and scan the surrounding ground for glue bags. There's nothing. My mind wanders back to the day in the museum with Pat. Pat who is now dead. Soon I'll be dead too. Maybe the museum was open that day to show us not to be afraid of being dead, because someone, somewhere knew that our time was nearly up. It seems to make sense.

To the side of me, I notice a large scorch mark on the log tree. I'd say someone has tried to set fire to it. It never used to be scarred because I remember checking before to see if it had been hit by lightning. I rub my fingers across the char - they go black. Maybe it's been struck by lightning recently, but I'd say it was kids trying to start a huge fire. The same kind of kids that gouged the lamb's eye out. Everything gets blamed on kids because they're seen as destructive and evil. That's how grownups get away with everything. They always blame stuff on kids and here I am doing the same. It could quite easily have been an adult's finger that ruined the painting, as it could have been an adult that tried to set fire to the log. From what I've discovered, adults are crueller and eviler than children, yet they get away with it without even being accused.

My thoughts create urges to become a just and fair adult. To confront and expose the liars and the abusers, but I've made my mind up. I'm never going to be an adult - I'm going to kill myself.

I jump off the log and follow the little brook that flows from the lake, as I contemplate drowning myself. Tripping on a piece of bamboo, I kick it away and see it has a small net on the end of it. I pick it up in the hope that it might be of some use to me. I continue to follow the stream to a spot clear of shrubbery, and I walk down the bank to the water's edge. Staring into the water, I imagine breathing it in. Then I spot a little fish, then another. A strange urge takes over my thoughts and I swipe the net through the water. A tiny silvery flickering fish is in the corner of the net. I caught one, but what to do with it? Laying the cane down, so the net is in the water, I scurry through the bushes looking for something to home my fish in. I spot what look likes a plastic sweet jar - the kind Mr. Brown has in his shop. It was probably stolen from his shop by one of the dope heads - they do eat a lot of stuff. It's caught in a bush, full of dead leaves and mud, but I manage to reach it, with minor scratches to my arms, and take it back to the bank. Once rinsed in the stream, I scoop up water which leaks from a crack in the side about half way down. Half a jar will have to do. I carefully flip the net over the jar, and my little fish plops into the water looking stunned.

As the murk in the stream clears, I wait for the next little fish to appear. The more I stare, the more fish I spot. Jab after jab, I strike to catch the little buggers. They are quick, but not as quick as me, and soon I have three more to join my little friend; I can't tell them apart though. Another jab and the cane snaps leaving me with a piece of stick. I watch the other end wash away downstream, and get stuck in an overhanging bush. I'm not going to be beaten. I wade into the shallow water, sinking in the muddy bottom. Trudging quickly so as not to get stuck, I reach out and grab the cane. The net tugs on the streambed, so I tug harder. It releases and I drag it back to the bank. It's full of slimy mud, and something is moving in it. I dip the net into the water to wash away the mud. I fish out the lumps of rotten leaf with my hand. Something wriggles between my fingers. Thinking it's a fish, I cup it in my hand and shake the dirty water away. A crawling sensation tickles the palm of my hand. I open my hand slowly and let out a scream, throwing the creature back into the water. I want to run, but my foot is stuck in the mud. I pull at my leg and as my boot is released the ground lets out a gurgling squelch. My boot is black with oily slime.

I check my hand to see if I've been bitten. I don't know what the creature was - it could be poisonous - maybe I should find somewhere to lie down and die. It looked like it could have been venomous. It was two inches long, black with loads of legs and big eyes like a baby dragon. It didn't bite me though, so I'll have to think of another way. My curiosity wants to know what the creature was, but it doesn't really matter because I'll be dead soon. I've lost my appetite for fishing, but I am hungry and thirsty. I sit down on the bank and bang my left leg on the ground trying to shake off some of the slime. Lifting my jar of fish to study them in detail, I see that one is floating on the surface and another is struggling to swim on its side. I feel sick; sick that I've trapped and imprisoned them, and that one of them is dead. I get up and pour them back into the stream. I came here to kill myself, instead I've killed some poor innocent little fish that was happily swimming around, causing nobody any harm an hour or so ago.

Telling myself what a horrible, useless, evil

person I must be, I leave the bank and make my way back to the tree log. My wet boots collect mud and sand from the track making them bigger and heavier with every step. I stop a couple of times to stamp it off, but by the time I'm back at the log there is no boot to be seen. I sit on the broken tree and stare at my feet. It's a shame they aren't caked in concrete. I could wait for it to dry and jump in the lake.

My feet have been freezing since they got wet, but I ignored them. Now my body is feeling as cold. I could just stay here on the log. It's a clear day, so it'll be a clear night which means it'll be freezing. I'll die of hypothermia. I can switch off the feeling of the pain, and my body will slowly close down. It'll be like going to sleep.

I turn my mind off and sit in a trancelike state with my eyes closed, for I don't know how long. I'm disturbed by the rustling of bushes. Opening my eyes I watch the bushes in front of me part. Adrenalin rushes through me and I'm on high alert again.

Earl appears in the opening, his fishing box over his shoulder. He sniggers, drops his kit on the ground and jumps up onto the log beside me.

"What happened to your hair?"

I can't believe it. I've been missing for days and he's laughing at my hair.

He opens a small container and takes out a large roll-up cigarette and a lighter.

"What are you doing?" I ask, as he lights it

and puffs out smoke rings.

"Have some of this."

"No. I don't smoke."

"Nor do I." He holds it out to me and I get a whiff of cannabis.

"For fuck's sake Earl - it's weed. You're only ten."

"Eleven. I was Eleven two days ago."

"Oh. I'm sorry I missed your birthday, but even so …"

"I blame you. I have to pretend that I spend my wages on maggots and stuff, so I have money to burn." He chuckles, and then he giggles and then he giggles some more. It's unbearable, so I take the joint from him and smoke it myself, until we're both laughing so much we can hardly breathe.

One joint after another appears.

"Did anyone notice I was missing?"

"No. Dad told us to tell everyone that you're sick with flu."

"What about Mum?"

"He told her that you've run away to create a scene and get attention. He says you won't last a week, and you'll be back home with your tail between your legs." He laughs and makes a whimpering sound like a pathetic dog.

"The wanker. I'll fucking show the bastard that I'm not a wuss." It's a strange sensation to be so angry while laughing so much.

"You won't get the chance to. Cos' I'm gonna kill him," Earl says with a huge grin on his face.

"Yeah. How?"

"I don't know for sure, but I'm going to. I bought a knife in the fishing shop. I think I'll just keep it on me until the next time he decides to pull me down the stairs or throw me around. Then I'll pull it out and stick it in his neck. Right there." He does a mime stabbing me in the throat with an imaginary knife.

"And I'll rush in and crouch behind him, then you can push him over before he can grab the knife and kill us back. You can have another go, into his heart once he's down. We'll blame it on a burglar."

"I don't want to blame it on a burglar. I want everyone to know it was me."

"But then you'll go to prison?"

"I'm eleven. I won't go to prison."

"We'll say it was both of us then. Two people can't murder a person, so we'll both be let off cos they won't be able to prove which one of us did it." I really don't want to go to prison, but I don't want Earl to either.

"Anyhow we should be going back. It's starting to get dark."

"Um. We? Haven't you forgotten something?"

"Don't be daft. They're expecting you, and we've got a deal."

"Where am I gonna say I've been?"

"Here. Tell them you've been hiding in the park all along. No one's been looking for you. I knew where to find you though."

Earl jumps down from the log and hoists his fishing box over his shoulder. I follow him through the bushes into the blackness.

Part 3 - Across The Universe, 2010.

My mobile is ringing. Opening my eyes I see the ceiling. Not the familiar one of my bedroom, and I'm on a hard floor with one leg up on a stool. My head is sore and I realise I must have fallen off the stool. Rising to my feet, I stretch and rub the bump on the back of my head - bloody vodka.

There are three missed calls on my phone - from Colin. I wonder how many it will take, for him to get the message that I'm not interested. Maybe I should do the decent thing and call him back - tell him that I'm too busy or that I'm not interested in seeing him again, but I shouldn't be talking to anyone in this drunken state. He is a lovely man, but he isn't aware of what I'm soon going to be faced with. The local paper will run the story, and there are plenty of people that'll know it concerns me. It would be impossible to hide it from him, and even harder to explain it all to him, so he's best to keep out of it. He'll give up soon enough. I need to do this on my own and who knows how long it'll drag on for?

Still a bit wobbly, from the bump and the vodka, I put on my coat and leave my house for some fresh air and some thinking time. Walking gives me the space I need to untangle my thoughts. The further I go, the better I feel. Sadly I can't walk away forever, and returning always has the reverse effect. Not knowing where I'm heading, I walk the length of my street, turn right at the end and keep going.

Looking back to the days of freedom that I had as a child, I'm quite disgusted about the way I dealt with it. It's not in my nature to act in such a depraved fashion. Putting it into perspective though, it wasn't really that terrible. I only had seven full days of freedom without Richard's involvement. That's one week out of ten years. One tiny week of rebellion in a decade of control and imprisonment, and I don't regret a minute of it. I'm sure it saved my life and my sanity at the time. I'm proud of myself for trying; it's all I could have done at the time.

I have friends now who know a little of what happened to me as a child. I think they've all asked the same eight word question at some point.

'Why didn't you say something at the time?' It's such a simple question to ask, but the answer is so much more difficult. These days they use words like grooming. I don't like this word; it sounds like you get lovingly brushed and stroked into submission. The truth is far from it. The process is about bringing you to your lowest to brainwash you into believing that the paedophile is invincible while you are dispensable, and no one in the world cares; in fact, the world will be a better place without you.

How can I answer such a question briefly? It's one that no-one actually wants to hear explained. When the question is asked, the expected response is a shrug of the shoulders and an 'I dunno.' Also it's not much of a conversation, with little debate for anyone who hasn't been through it. Anyone that has lived through it and does understand would not ask the question in the first place.

Even when I've tried to get across the basics to people who have listened they say things like, "So you can't like sex then? You must be a man hater." I made up a little analogy to explain this, rather than merely deny it and not be believed.

'Imagine all men are wasps and bees. They all have wings, six hairy legs, two black antenna sticking out of the top of their heads, yellow and black stripes, and a sting in their abdomens. They sound like the same creature when I describe their features, but there is a difference. It's one that you find out the hard way and should learn to recognise. The wasp wants to sting you and hurt you, through no fault of your own, purely for its own gratification. Whereas the bee has no intension of hurting you. All the bee wants to do is make sweet honey. One wasp sting isn't going to stop me liking honey.'

There are good and evil people in the world and those in between - women as well as men - and I'm not going to let one beast that ruined my childhood also ruin my adulthood.

That is easier to say than to believe, but I have continued to strive to convince myself of this.

Always Crashing in the Same Car

The sky is darkening, yet I have no idea of the time, or how long I was out cold on the floor after my little mishap. It doesn't matter to me; I've made sure time doesn't concern me. My house has no clocks. Any gadgets that do shine the time at me, like the cooker or my mobile, are set wrong, and I avoid learning how wrong. If I need to know the exact time, I have a button on my answer-phone. A nice lady's voice tells me what time it is without me having to see a clock. I even chose the house I live in because - on looking at the view from the rear window - I could see a church, and its clock showed the time as twenty-to-two. It wasn't correct, and has always shown twenty-to-two. It made everything perfect. If it's ever repaired, I'll have to move house.

Aware that my walk was not aimless, and some deep psychological motive has brought me to this spot outside a college, I stop for a second before turning and walking up the steps of the building. I trip, but don't fall. As I look to see if anyone saw my drunken stumble, I sit down in an effort to disguise it.

This is the college where I spent three months studying Graphic Design - only a short while, but for good reason.

The day Earl and I left the park and headed home with a plan to get rid of Richard forever, was the last day that I had any soul. We didn't execute our scheme to finish him off. I never got the chance to rebel, dilute, escape or fight back. Taking it out on myself I would cut the skin on my arms and even my face, in the hope that someone would see the damage that was being done on the inside. Nobody did. I waited in silence in the small dark place in the back of mind - with only David Bowie to comfort me - for one, two then three very long years. Aged seventeen, I'd found myself in this college with a four year course ahead of me. It hadn't been my choice; it was Richard's way of keeping me for eternity. The little spark of me, that remained, was less than dormant.

The students in my class were all complete strangers to me, and I was quite happy to let it stay that way. They weren't like me, and I believed they wouldn't have liked me. I left them to their childish pranks, stupid romances and unfolding dramas. They all thought they were so grown up. Some of them had cars, and they went to parties at the weekends. They'd get drunk, fall down stairs, get high, throw up and crack their heads open on sinks. They would talk about it all week in lectures - how great it had all been. I didn't feel left out. To me they were incredibly childish; they should have grown out of it long ago. They had the chance to be grown up, but were acting like kids. I really wanted to be a grown-up and even though I was old enough to be one, I still wasn't.

Sitting in my own little world in class, I'd blanked any approaches from people trying to make conversation. Instead I would fantasise about blowing the college up. It would have been a huge explosion that would have left body parts splattered everywhere - making it impossible to identify everybody. The fire would have consumed most of them, and I'd have been the only survivor, leaving Richard to believe I was dead. Then I'd be free.

I hadn't even tried to sneak out at lunchtimes. It wasn't worth the trouble I'd get in.

For weeks, I sat in silence and got on with my work - bothered by no one - until one lunchtime, I was joined at my table by Matthew.

"Hi. There's a party on Saturday night at my mate's house. I was just wondering if you wanted to come."

Pretending I hadn't heard him, I got up and walked hurriedly away. I feared I'd been spotted by some external force for committing the crime of corresponding with another person.

After that day, Matthew always made a point of saying hello to me even though I didn't respond. This bizarre carry-on continued for weeks until the day after a very bad night with Richard, and all because the photography teacher had sent us into town, on our own, to photograph buildings.

Bending down, bruised and aching, I was shoving some stuff into my locker. Matthew walked past me, "Hello you," he said, not expecting a response.

"Hello," I whispered.

As the words left my mouth, fright and vulnerability struck me. I closed my locker, my heart was thumping and I speed-walked through the corridor afraid that the ceiling would fall in and crash down on my head. Then I was angry with myself. Why had I said that? Having answered him once I'd have had to answer him again. My defence had been broken, so instead I avoided him. When I saw him in a corridor, I'd dive into the nearest room or cupboard. I couldn't keep it up for long though, and he soon caught me with my head in my locker again.

"You do know everyone here thinks you're up your own arse - that you think you're better than the rest of us, don't you?"

I couldn't believe what I was hearing. It was totally the opposite of how I saw things. I had to respond.

"I'm sorry, and I don't think that at all."

"You don't need to be sorry, and believe me, I don't think that you're like that. Everyone else does though." He walked away leaving me with that thought, and a terrible feeling that something was about to crack me over the head for replying. When nothing had happened, and my head was still intact, I realised the fear was all Richard's doing. He couldn't see me, he couldn't attack me and he didn't know who I'd spoken to. He'd merely made me believe he could do all these things. It was all in my mind, and so was I - somewhere in the far reaches, deep at the back.

Mat started sitting with me at lunch times, and I started looking forward to it and overcoming the fear. The impression I got of him was that he was a bit weird in a creepy way, but what did I know? Everyone I had ever met seemed weird to me. I thought maybe it was me that was strange.

I didn't say a lot at first. We talked about class mostly. He was on the same course, but two years ahead of me. He offered to help me with my work, but I wasn't interested in my work. I didn't want to be at the college. It was another prison, and I had no intentions of sticking it out for four hellish years.

His questions soon turned to what my others interests were ; what I did out of college. I'd made up some rubbish that I painted murals. It was the first thing that came into my head. I know he was only trying to make conversation, but to me it was like an interrogation, and I'm sure I made up loads of lies to fill in the blankness of my life. Talking to him still made me nervous, and my skin would burn and sting, but I needed his company, and could ignore the irritation after a while.

I'm glad Mat continued to persevere with me however it turned out. He sat beside me one lunchtime and asked a simple question. "Do you fancy coming for a drink in the Uni bar later? It's just that it's my birthday and I'm going out with some mates tonight. I know you won't be interested in meeting them, but maybe me and you could have some time after college."

"I can't, sorry, but happy birthday." I had to refuse. I had no choice in anything that I did. I couldn't even ask for permission without reprisals. All that was important was to get home on time.

"Surely half an hour wouldn't hurt?"

If only he'd known how much half an hour would hurt. I refused again, and he looked genuinely upset. We sat in silence for a little while. I really wanted to go with him, and I should have been able to be like all the other students and make my own decisions. Richard's grip on me was ridiculous. I could see it myself more and more as the days passed. Mat could have asked anyone to go with him, and they'd have been able to say without any forethought, "Yes." A stirring of anger at the situation released a part of my old fighting self. The burst of rebellion frightened me at first, but so long as Mat stayed by my side, I was going to call home and ask for permission.

"Will you come to the phone with me? I have to call home, and I might be allo ... able to come with you later."

"Really? Of course I will."

How scared and exhilarated I was walking to the pay phone. On reaching it, I hesitated and doubted my intention. Mat had taken hold of my arm, then my hand.

"What's the matter with you? You're shaking like mad."

"Nothing I'm fine. Can I borrow twenty pence?"

Mat gave me the money and I picked up the receiver. Trembling terribly I dropped the twenty, as I hovered it over the slot. Mat picked it up as I tapped in the number. It beeped for a few seconds before Richard answered. I pushed Mat's hand to the slot and the twenty went in. He held my hand tight, aware that something was wrong, but bemused by my actions.

Richard recited the phone number before saying hello. In a gibbering voice I began to explain.

"I have to stay behind to finish a project. If it dries out before I've finished it'll be ruined. I might be about half an hour late home."

"Do you think I'm an imbecile? You won't be late MY girl. You'll be back here on time. You think I don't know what you're up to? Well I do. Woe betide you if you're late, MY girl…" I held the phone away from my ear, as the insults got worse. He was talking in his evil nasally voice, half laughing and half threatening.

Tears welled up in my eyes. Mat took the receiver from me and slammed it down.

"What the fuck is going on? Who were you talking to?"

"My stepdad, Richard."

"Are you serious? And you can't even tell him you're going to be late without making excuses?"

"He's a bit strict."

"That's rubbish. Look at the state of you."

I burst into floods of tears. Mat held me for a while without saying anything. I feared going home even more than before. I looked up to Mat and snotted out the words, "I don't want to go home."

"You're not going home. Come with me." He kept his arm around me as we walked out of the college and into the car park. He opened the door to a VW beetle.

"Where are we going?"

"Get in. I'm taking you to my house."

Sitting in the passenger seat I doubled up, resting my head on my knees. I was running and hiding again and terrified.

Strange thoughts swirled through my head as I was driven blindly through the town. I remembered the last time I'd escaped only to find myself back at that hell house and the repercussions of my disobedience. It occurred to me that I didn't know where Mat lived. He could live in the same street as me; dead opposite knowing my luck. I wouldn't be able to get out of the car. Literally, I wished his car would drive forever. I never wanted to get out of it.

The car slowed on the crunching of a gravel driveway. It stopped; we didn't seem to have gone far.

"You can sit up now. Come on let's get inside."

"Can you go and open the front door first?"

"Sure." Mat left the car and returned to open the passenger door. Climbing out, I ducked down and ran into the house. He followed me and locked the door. We sat in the kitchen, and he made coffee. He wanted to know what was so terrible at home, but I didn't want to tell him. He might not have believed me, he might have thought that I was crazy, or a liar, and send me away. Even if I had told him the truth, and he'd believed me, it might have made him angry. He might have gone and done something that would make it even worse.

"Look you don't have to tell me now, but I can tell that it must be something pretty horrendous. You can stay here in my room for as long as you like. My dad's posted in Germany for two years, so I could do with some company. Don't worry."

"I'm worried for my brother, my sister and my mum. He'll be so angry if I don't go home."

"The only person you need to worry about is you right now. You can ring your mum from here, and tell her you're okay but won't be coming home. We don't want a missing person hunt."

"My mum doesn't answer the phone. Richard does, and I can't speak to him again."

"You are seventeen years old. You can do whatever you want. Come on, you're going to ring him and tell him you're not going home. Don't listen to anything he says to persuade you to go back. You can say no can't you? Say it."

We sat at the bottom of the stairs together. Mat held the receiver to my head. As I pressed the buttons, I didn't feel so safe in the house anymore. Within a few seconds Richard would be in the house too, in the phone. Trembling I listened as the call was picked up.

Before Richard had the chance to recite the number, I was squeezed tightly by Mat and managed to say, "I'm never coming back." I didn't want to hear his reply, so slammed the phone down. I'd done it.

Hiding in Mat's room while he was at college, I lived in fear of every knock at the door and every bump from the neighbours' house. When Mat was there I felt safe, and we planned to move far away when he'd finished college. All I had to do was wait a couple of years.

That was the last day I'd walked up these college steps until today. I'm so different now compared to that wreck-of-a-girl that once came here. It's almost hard to believe that it was me.

I saw a science program, some years back, that explained that every cell in your body reproduces and dies every five years. It made me see that my entire body is a different one to the one that Richard messed with. He has never touched this body. As far as I know, he's never even laid eyes on this body. It's kind of a shame that the memories don't die too, but then how would I recall it all in court without them? Everything seems to have worked out perfectly, and I love being a grown up.

I rise from the steps to continue my walk. I really fancy another drink, so I head off in search of a pub.

Scream Like a Baby

Walking away from the college, it dawns on me that it has been over twenty years since Mat and I set up house together. I must be classed as old now. Only old people say 'oh, it was about twenty years ago when...' like it is no time at all. I wonder what I must look like - an old drunken woman wandering along in the dark in search of a pub. It's not the best impression to make, but today I don't care. I have a reason to celebrate, and I'll stay out all night, and get as drunk as I like if I choose too because I'm a grown up, and an old one at that.

It's quite unbelievable how fast the last two decades have passed. The first twenty years of my life were more like a hundred years with every day dragging on by the second.

My son is now twenty-one years old. His childhood has gone in a flash; he's a man now. The same age as I was when I found out he was growing inside me.

It was on a cold October morning, and I'd woken feeling strangely sick. Not the kind of sick like when you're ill, or have eaten something bad. It was the same sickness you get when you read a book on a car journey. It happened again the next morning and the next. Frying some bacon one evening, I puked on the kitchen floor without any warning.

Mat got me a home pregnancy test, and it was confirmed. I had never worried about getting pregnant; I assumed that I couldn't. Surely if I could have, I'd have got pregnant long before then. Believing that I must have been damaged somehow as I child, I had taken no precautions with Mat.

Because Richard used to tell me that he'd get it sorted if I ever did get pregnant, I not only had diluting him on my brain, but also diluting the chance that if I did get pregnant it wouldn't be by him. I never believed that Richard had been talking of abortion - that wouldn't have been productive for him - I'm sure he thought of it as another way to keep me in his grasp and in his hell house. It was more likely that he planned to imprison me for longer - tied to him with a child - unable to ever escape.

Logically I'd known, the child was Mat's. I hadn't seen or heard from Richard in over two years, and I hadn't been with anyone else, but something niggled in my mind. I didn't trust anyone, not even Mat, and throughout the pregnancy I wondered if Richard might have paid him money to somehow get his sperm into me. Not being able to mention the ludicrous notion to Mat, the idea grew in my mind, as the child grew inside me.

I'd made one trip to the doctor to tell him I was pregnant after about six months, at Mat's insistence, the doctor agreed with me. The journey to the surgery was as bad as the day I'd left the college in the Beetle. I hid behind Mat in the waiting room, clinging to his arm like a frightened child. It wasn't only me at stake anymore. I had this little person inside me to protect from the forces of evil that I imagined were all around me.

On the journey home, Mat had mentioned that I might want to get some mental help. Laughing it off, I'd convinced him that I'd be fine once the baby was born, and it was left at that.

The pains began on the hottest day of the year. I tried to hide them, but being already eleven days overdue, Mat was being extra vigilant. He managed to get me into the car and to the hospital, where I refused to get out. He went inside and got some staff to help. That walk across the car park was worse than any of the nightmares I'd been encountering. Fear of something hitting me from the sky, or a motorbike riding into me, left me unable to walk, as well as the pain of the contractions.

Somehow they got me inside. They wanted me to lie on a bed, but I refused. They pushed and pinned me down while I screamed and fought to get away. They strapped my legs up in the air and stuck a needle in my arse. I stopped struggling, listening to their voices. They were talking in code to each other, so I wouldn't understand. I tried to focus on them, but the room had become distorted.

A man's face hovered over my own. He was talking in a drone that I couldn't understand.

Unable to wriggle free, I tried to focus on his face. It looked like it was reflected from a metal spoon. His nose grew, turning bright red like a clown's. Then it popped like a soap bubble, and the little bits of wetness splattered on my face. I found the energy to scream and struggle again, as I felt things intruding in my undercarriage. I glimpsed a sight of Mat across the room, and screamed out for him to help me. His face looked as terrified, as I truly was. Then he was gone. I pulled at the edges of the bed desperately trying to free myself, but it was too late - the people had all got inside me somehow. I could feel them tunnelling in and walking around inside my body. I pushed against them, harder and harder, determined to force them out. One last scream and I felt them expelled in one massive squelching heap. Relieved and gasping for breath I believed I'd killed them, until someone tapped me on the cheek and something landed on my chest. The voices were still inaudible. Opening my eyes, I looked down to my chest. Seeing the baby alien from the film 'Alien', I let out a louder scream, and I swiped at the monster to get it away from me. It was quickly removed by one of the people, its jaws snapping at me as it disappeared from view.

    Exhausted I slipped into sleep, awaking to the sight of florescent, tubular lights passing over me on the ceiling. Was I floating? No, someone was pushing me. I looked at the man at the foot of the bed who was wheeling me like a baby in a pram. I was safe. He wasn't an alien - I believed he was

Benny from the soap opera - Crossroads. I told him he was stupid to give all his money to a donkey home, and I went back to sleep completely unaware that I'd had a baby.

I was awoken by a huge black nurse leaning over me. I didn't know where I was. She was holding a baby in one hand and my right breast in her other. "You have to feed your baby."

Afraid I was having a nightmare, I closed my eyes again. She fed the baby from my boob and then transferred it to the other while I got my head around the situation. When she'd gone I looked around the room. I was in a ward with loads of other women. There was a fish tank next to my bed with a baby in it. Stroking my flattened tummy, I realised the child was mine. My instinct told me to get up and get home, taking the tot with me, but I couldn't even sit up, and had to spend a whole week in the hospital, afraid of visiting time, or an open window, barely sleeping at all. I was told I'd had an overreaction to the Pethidine they had injected into my arse without my consent. I believe they gave me the wrong dose. I never heard of anyone that had a reaction like mine.

When I did get home, I found Mat had bought a red pushchair. He kept putting the baby in it, and telling me to take it for a walk. He handed me 'mums and tots' leaflets and tried to encourage me to get out while he was at work. Getting more frustrated with me, he threatened to go to my doctor himself and tell him that I was mental. He said if I didn't get help they might take the baby away.

Realising he was serious, I knew I had to do something to ease the pressure on us both. I started ordering stuff from the milkman: potatoes, butter, eggs, cheese and anything else he sold, so I could pretend that I'd taken the baby to the shops. I persuaded the milkman to bring me other stuff too which he was happy to oblige. He was making money and I got less hassle from Mat. The nice man even sold me nappies. I hated having to open the front door in the morning to take in the shopping, but a bigger letterbox would have been too dangerous. Even doing any kind of housework, that made a noise, had become impossible. Switching on the hoover brought on terrible anxiety, making me think that someone was breaking into the house while I couldn't hear.

I was convinced life would be easier if we could move away from that town, but Mat had got a good job and he had no intentions of moving away. I coped with how it was, blind to the fact that Mat had had enough of me. He was acting quite content.

Believing I had it all under control and everything was fine, I was shocked to hear something fall through the letter box at an unexpected time. It was the local newspaper. Staring at it lying on the floor, I ran through the reasons why someone might post it to me. Discarding my paranoid thoughts, I guessed that the paper boy had delivered it to the wrong house. To avoid him returning or a neighbour come knocking, looking for it, I decided to push it back through the letter box. On picking it up I was surprised to see a photo of Mat on the front. Someone had purposefully delivered it to me. The headline read: 'Police crackdown on curb crawlers", or something to that effect. The following article was about how the Police were cleaning the streets of prostitutes by targeting curb crawlers, taking them to court, and naming and shaming them in the local paper. The culprit this time was Mat. The story described him being caught in his work van with a prostitute performing a sexual act. Strangely I wasn't that shocked, just disappointed. I had no illusions that anyone was an angel, and I had always had my suspicions that Mat was slightly weird. I thought I'd mention it to him when he got home from work.

Within minutes of reading the whole article, the telephone rang. I was unsure whether to answer it. The only person who ever rang the house was Mat's mum. I thought maybe she'd seen the paper. I answered the phone.

"Hello."

"Hi, my name's Nicky. I just wanted to say that it was me that put the paper through your door."

"Who are you?"

"I'm Mat's girlfriend, or I was until I saw that. I thought you should know about it."

"What the prostitute thing or that he's got a girlfriend?"

"Both. I just want you to know that I won't be seeing him anymore. He's been telling me for months that he'd leave you if he could, but he's afraid that you'll commit suicide if he does. I believed him, but this prostitute stuff is disgusting, and I'm gonna make sure he knows it. You should seriously get a grip of yourself and kick him into touch too if you've got any sense."

"Er … okay. Thanks for letting me know." I hung up.

I couldn't understand why she had told me all that especially if she believed I was suicidal. It seemed very irresponsible. She also seemed a lot more upset about the whole thing than I was. The prostitute thing hadn't bothered me in the slightest; the fact that he'd been telling people that I couldn't live without him had pissed me off big time. I'd survived worse than that shit, and I wasn't ready to jump off a cliff for him. I was angry with myself for getting into the whole situation. Things had to change and I was one of them.

It's strange to think that, once upon a time, I was scared of the letter box opening, whereas now I'm wandering the dark streets alone.

Crossing the road to a pub I once worked in, I am disappointed to find that its windows are boarded up. I check the door in the hope it's still open, but it's not. Another one closed for good. Whoever came up with the idea to ban smoking in pubs should be shot. Every week another pub closes and more people stay at home, locked in. It's not good for their souls or for the community.

Turning away from the door I head off in search of another.

It's No Game

Discovering the revelations about Mat and ditching him was the best thing I could have done. It opened my eyes to the life I was leading and the state I'd got into. If I'd stayed with him things would only have gone further downhill.

I went to the doctor of my own accord. I knew that I hadn't come into this world damaged and screwed up in the head. If something can be done then it can be undone. I broke down in the surgery and found where to begin impossible. He told me to go home and write everything down on paper, and send it to him before making another appointment. What I wrote surprised me.

I explained about my upbringing, about the nightmares causing my lack of sleep and disturbing my mind, and I wrote of the darkness, and how I felt guilty about my thoughts of dying, what with a child that depended on me. I realised while writing the letter that I had a serious problem. I was having suicidal thoughts, not the kind of thoughts I'd had when I'd wanted to kill myself at fourteen years old. This was something completely different. At fourteen I had been angry. Killing myself was more of a violent punishment to me and to a world that betrayed me.

The desolation of myself and my soul was responsible for the place I was at in my twenties. I didn't want to actually kill myself; I already felt dead. I had lost my will, but I knew I had to get a grip. I couldn't carry on living like that. I was gutted that the strong little mind I'd once had, had turned on me at the time.

When I returned to the doctor he said very little, but referred me to a psychotherapist. I was pleased that he hadn't prescribed me pills to lift my spirits. I knew I needed help not a plaster, and so did he.

Starting the sessions, I was determined to get better, but I was totally unaware of how these things worked. She'd ask me questions about the nightmares, and I'd answer as best I could. I began to think it a waste of time - what had the images in my dreams got to do with all the damage that had been caused and the low, dark place that my head was in? Having a set appointment once, then twice a week, I continued and slowly things started to change. I became aware that I was dreaming, while I was actually fast asleep. When I'd dreamt that I was trying to run away from a monster, when I'd felt like I was running hopelessly in sand and getting nowhere, and when I'd tried to scream but no noise would come out of my mouth, I'd become lucid.

These occurrences became the triggers to controlling the outcome of the nightmares. These recurring incidents during dreaming brought on a state of consciousness. I was fully aware that I was dreaming, although I was still sound asleep. I could fight to wake myself up, or turn the dream to my advantage. This lucid dreaming made me invincible. I could walk through war zones - I could be shot at or blown up and just keep on walking - I could fight rapists and call up armies to be on my side, nothing could touch me. Of course, it didn't always work and doesn't to this day. Sometimes in a deeper sleep or with less alcohol in me, I don't become aware that I'm dreaming at all and I'm just a child again, reliving the past events over and over again with no control of it until I wake with a shout or a scream, sweating and shaking and too frightened even to open my eyes.

Somehow, every session where I talked about my nightmares, got on to the topic of one thing or another about the time I lived with Richard. There wasn't a particular day that the fog lifted, but it did.

I used to think that it was a shame that I had no memories before the age of five or six. It would have been much nicer to dream about those times before Richard appeared. I turned it to my advantage in later life. If I'm ever asked about my childhood, I refer to those particular younger years as wonderful, exciting, free and full of love and sunshiny days. It might well have been like that before I was six, it might not have, but it is my fantastic, fantasy childhood. It can be used as if it were my whole childhood, and it plays a big part in my psychological well-being today. I hardly ever talk about the other ten or so years after it. *My real childhood*.

I really shouldn't be thinking about my

imaginary childhood, or all the escapes I got up to while living with Richard. And I really shouldn't be wandering the streets in search of an open pub in the hope of getting completely wasted, instead of going home and concentrating on the real issues that I'm going to have to deal with in court.

It's a horrible thought that I have to recall everything. Everything down to the minutest detail that I don't want to think about ever again. I have to actually relive all that shit and tell total strangers about it. I know it's all in here. The nightmares remind me, but they twist it all too. I want it to go away, but it will never go away because it is in me, it is part of me, it is what helped make me who I am, and how fucking angry I am deep inside.

The judge and jury are not going to be interested in the nightmares just the truth, the whole truth and nothing but the truth. I have it all in my memory for eternity. I will share it with them, and whoever else is present including the nosy people in the public gallery. It isn't going to be easy, but I knew this day would come. I have been waiting - I am ready for it. I needed this day to come and I'm sure the others feel the same.

Spotting the bright lights of a pub in the distance, I think how uncanny it is that I'll be ending the day in the same place that I started the journey that resulted in the phone call this morning.

I'd been in there on a hen night, it must be over two years ago now. It was for some girl from work that I hardly knew. We'd all got quite drunk and were having a really good harmless laugh together. The conversation turned to the subject of the age that each of us had lost our virginities, who with and how good or bad it had been. I made my excuses that I needed the loo - I had to leave their company before it got round to my turn. My skin was beginning to sting at the very first mention of it. Instead of returning to their table, I loitered at the other side of the bar waiting for the conversation to move on. I got chatting to a guy called Andrew and we decided to meet up in the week.

To cut things short, Andrew and I went out together a few times, and after a couple of months, I found myself back at his place and a bit tipsy. He was nice, but I couldn't see a lasting relationship coming out of it.

He managed to get me into his bed that night. I knew I wasn't entirely happy about it - it didn't seem like the right time. I still wasn't sure how much I liked him. I knew I didn't love him. Thinking it was my own demons trying to get in the way, I ignored my instincts and went with the flow.

I thought everything was going right until he pushed me away and angrily said, "God you're so rigid, why don't you relax? It's like trying to have sex with a child!"

That comment hit home more than any psychotherapy, more than any drunken arse-hole in a pub telling me that I had a fucking attitude problem, and more than any late night chats with the Samaritans. I was exposed - maybe he knew. It was a horrid moment. I didn't answer him. I got out of bed, dressed and left. He didn't say a word or try to stop me.

I couldn't believe it; I was forty years old and being told that fucking me was like fucking a child. It had crossed my mind that maybe I didn't know how to fuck like a grown-up and maybe that was why Mat did what he did. And the biggest maybe of all - why I wasn't in a stable relationship like most normal people. Was it because no one had ever had the guts to say that fucking me was like fucking a child? I'd shuddered at the thought of wondering how Andrew knew what it was like to fuck a child; God was he a paedophile?

Not sleeping at all that night, I'd become angrier and angrier. I believed I'd done all I could do to put the past behind me, but Richard was still free. Free from blame, free to do it to someone else. Free to make me live with the regret that I had never exposed him for the rest of my life. There was only one thing to do about it, and it was the scariest moment of my life.

The following morning I'd called the police station and asked to speak to a woman officer. She made an appointment with me for an interview at the station. That was over two years ago. Two years I've been waiting for the call that I received this morning. It's hard to grasp the fact that Richard is finally sitting in a police cell not far from here.

I did something else that morning. I booked a helicopter lesson, but that's another story.

Pushing open the pub door, I get a whiff of piss and stale sweat. Pubs never smelt like this before the smoking ban.

After All

I've worked in many pubs over the years, never being afraid of the crowds of drunken men. Together they aren't a threat to me. It's only when I'm alone with one that my skin itches, but that's only mildly irritating.

Looking around the bar, I don't see anyone I recognise for sure. Every pub has the same crowd and the same characters. They are merely in different bodies. I've learnt not to sit at a table on my own, as the soberest guys will soon encourage one of the drunkest ones to join me, and try his luck, while they laugh at him. So, I walk straight up to the crowd and even though there isn't a spare stool, I prop myself up against the bar. I don't care if they think I'm a prostitute or a lush. I can see them and hear what they're saying from here. It also gives me an air of confidence.

The barmaid seems in no hurry, so I hold out a fiver to catch her attention as I hate it when people tap coins on the bar.

"Yes?"

Um, not the most welcoming request.

"Double vodka, lime and soda please."

"D'ya want ice?"

"No thanks."

I pay for my drink, staying where I am, glancing up at the telly. The guy closest to me apologises and gets off of his stool offering it to me. "No, it's okay. I'm fine standing," I reply.

"I insist. I've been sitting on my arse all day. I could do with a stretch." He carries on his conversation with his fellow drinkers. As he's not going to sit back down on the stool, I politely take it and say thanks. They are so predictable.

My drink is gone in seconds, so I catch the girl's attention again by holding up my empty glass. She's texting or playing Angry Birds on her phone, and she looks displeased at the interruption.

"Same again?"

"Yeah, but less lime. That was a bit strong."

She serves me and goes back to her mobile.

Drinking it, I'd say she's put more lime in it than she did the first time, so I swig down half the glass and call her back.

"Hey. Excuse me."

She slams her mobile down and marches back, staring at me with her head at an angle.

"Could you top this up with soda please. There's too much lime in it."

She sprays soda up to the top of the glass and bangs it back on the bar slopping it onto the beer mat.

Now, I've been a barmaid and I always found that you could have a good crack with the customers. It's much more enjoyable than being a stroppy cow. I wonder if she's getting some bad shit from someone on her phone; I start to feel sorry for her. She's only young and who knows what kind of life she leads outside of here. Maybe she's really upset and angry like I was at her age. Maybe she'll be standing this side of the bar in twenty years' time after receiving a similar phone call to the one I had this morning. It's a horrible thought that there are children out there who are suffering now with what I went through so long ago.

The guy standing next to me seems to have noticed that I'm watching her.

"She's not good is she? Spoilt little rich girl and she wonders why she never gets bought a drink."

"She might be unhappy about something," I reply in her defence.

"Yeah. She's unhappy alright. Daddy's making her earn her own money while she's away from home, studying at Uni to be a lawyer or something. She fucking hates working here. She'd rather be at home with Mummy and Daddy bending over backwards for her. Stuck up little princess."

I find his theory very hard to relate to. Why would anyone want to live with their parents when they have the chance of freedom, education and a future. I stop feeling sorry for her, and try to catch her attention again. She's off the phone, but now filing her nails.

I clink a coin against my glass. I don't care that it's rude and annoying anymore.

"Yes?"

"Would you put another double vodka in this please?"

"Do you want lime?"

"No. Just another double - there's enough lime in it."

"It doesn't look like there's any lime in it."

"Well there fucking is. Just put another double fucking vodka in it."

She does as I ask and disappears out the back. The guy next to me shakes his head and turns away.

When she reappears, she stands as far from me as she can, rubbing the file over her hand. A portly man appears next to her, and she nods towards me. He approaches me with a smile.

"Do you have a problem with something?"

"Yeah. There's too much lime in this." I take a swig from the glass and wince.

The man, who I've guessed is the landlord, takes the glass from me and holds it up to the light.

"It looks to me like there's no lime in this at all. In fact, it's as clear as water if you ask me." He puts it back down in front of me.

"Taste it. You'll see what I mean." I pick the drink up and hold it out to him.

"I'm sorry, but I'm not going to taste it." He's walking out from around the bar and I know what's coming. Every eye in the pub is now focused on me, and I'm pissed out of my tree. As he approaches me I gulp down most of what's left and spit a little back out in his direction before yelling at him.

"It might look clear to you, but it's still there.

I know it's there, and it's still bitter. It's bitter as fuck."

The landlord pulls me by my arm and drags me through the door, *throwing* me into the street.

"You're drunk. It's TIME you went HOME," he shouts at me.

On hearing those words, I freeze and wait for the expected surge of anger to be released.

Instead a long forgotten voice whispers in my head. *"Take your time - Enjoy your walk home Marie. After all, it's over now. You are believed."*

I turn to make my way back home. 'Thank you David. You can go now - and my name is Jes.'

Epilogue/Epitaph

Jes decided to write a book about her experience. Her wish is that one day it will be read by a parent, a teacher or any adult who might then recognise that a child known to them is in serious danger. Her hope is that this will encourage intervention, and prevent that child from living the same nightmare that she has.

Although this is Jes's story, many people have asked what happened to Richard.

Richard was arrested in November 2010. He remained in prison with a plea of not guilty until July 2011.

On that day, with the jury minutes away from being sworn in and the victims and witnesses expecting a long and painful trial, he changed his plea to guilty. He was sentenced to 15 years imprisonment.

He died of bowel cancer, in prison, in Sept 2012.

Printed in Great Britain
by Amazon